The Railway to Heaven

*From the UK to Tibet on the longest
and highest railways in the world*

Matthew Woodward

LANNA HALL PUBLISHING

A LANNA HALL BOOK

First published in Great Britain in 2019

by Lanna Hall Publishing

Copyright © 2019 Matthew Woodward

Matthew Woodward has asserted his right under
the Copyright, Designs and Patents Act 1988 to
be identified as the author of this work.

ISBN 978-1-98071-376-0

Cover design and maps by Colin Brooks

Illustrations by Olga Tyukova

Edited by Caroline Petherick

www.matthew-woodward.com

Travelling is a brutality.
It forces you to trust strangers and to lose sight
of all that familiar comfort of home and friends.
You are constantly off balance. Nothing is yours except
the essential things – air, sleep, dreams, the sea,
the sky – all things tending towards the eternal
or what we might imagine of it.

Cesare Pavese

Author's note: as most of the place names are translated into English from the Russian Cyrillic alphabet and Chinese characters, the versions vary between sources and over time. The spellings I've used in this book are those that were in the timetables published at the time of my journey

Contents

Introduction

Successful long-range rail adventure can sometimes feel like an exercise in planetary alignment. Cosmic events take place that you have absolutely no control over. Changes in economic and political circumstances allow exciting new routes to be explored, but at the same time others close, and often without much warning. Some amazing journeys that were once very normal have become virtually impossible. Take, for example, the route of the original Orient Express and Taurus Express. In 1940 it was possible to travel from London to Istanbul and onward to Baghdad by just two trains – more than 2500 miles (4000 km) through quite a lot of countries in less than eight days. But at the time of writing, even though we now have a tunnel under the English Channel, it is hard work connecting several infrequent trains to reach Istanbul, let alone onward to Iraq: underinvestment in infrastructure, red tape, engineering projects and of course civil war, often prevent the success of such an endeavour.

The start of this, my third, big rail adventure was driven by my desire to follow a Silk Route from Europe by train across the Middle East and onward into Asia. But the planets were not quite lined up and I had to consider alternatives. Something meaningful and challenging. In 2006 China managed to connect its highest province by train, when it opened the final stretch of the Qinghai–Tibet railway, reaching as far as Lhasa. Life in Tibet has been substantially influenced by the completion of this project; whatever your opinions on the geopolitical issues, the immensity of the civil engineering achievement is obvious to anyone who ascends the railway to heaven.

Who knows what might become possible in the future? It is now likely that the railway line will be extended from China into Nepal in the next few years, and even as far as India. If this happens an alternative Hippy Trail will become possible. We live in interesting times.

Matthew Woodward
Chichester, West Sussex, 2019

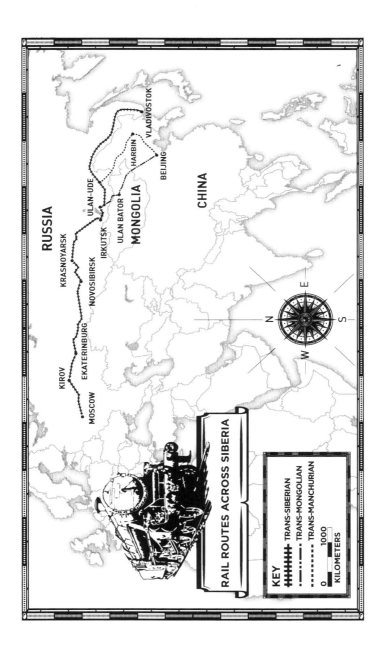

RAIL ROUTES ACROSS SIBERIA

KEY
TRANS-SIBERIAN
TRANS-MONGOLIAN
TRANS-MANCHURIAN

0   1000
KILOMETERS

RUSSIA

MOSCOW
KIROV
EKATERINBURG
KRASNOYARSK
NOVOSIBIRSK
IRKUTSK
ULAN-UDE
ULAN BATOR
MONGOLIA
HARBIN
BEIJING
VLADIVOSTOK
CHINA

N E S W

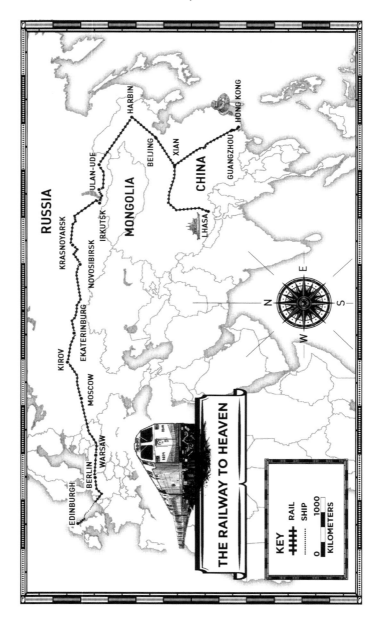

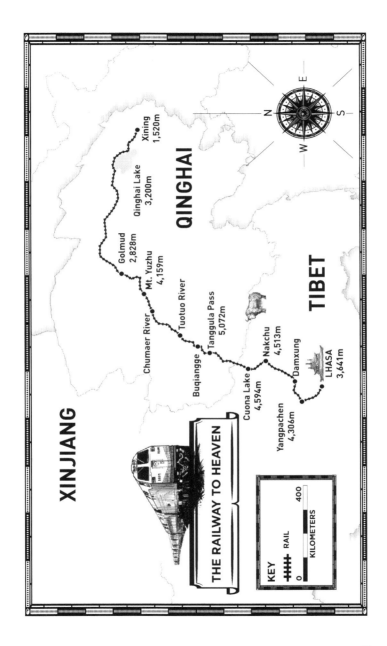

XINJIANG

QINGHAI

TIBET

Xining
1,520m

Qinghai Lake
3,200m

Golmud
2,828m

Mt. Yuzhu
4,159m

Chumaer River

Tuotuo River

Buqiangge

Tanggula Pass
5,072m

Nakchu
4,513m

Cuona Lake
4,594m

Damxung

Yangpachen
4,306m

LHASA
3,641m

THE RAILWAY TO HEAVEN

KEY

RAIL

0   400

KILOMETERS

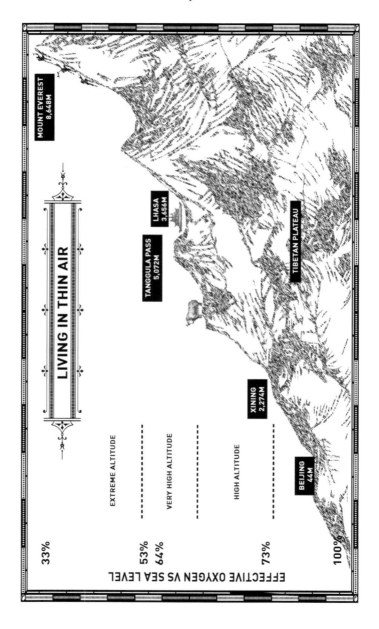

LIVING IN THIN AIR

MOUNT EVEREST
8,848M

LHASA
3,656M

TANGGULA PASS
5,072M

TIBETAN PLATEAU

XINING
2,274M

BEIJING
44M

EXTREME ALTITUDE

VERY HIGH ALTITUDE

HIGH ALTITUDE

EFFECTIVE OXYGEN VS SEA LEVEL

33%

53%
64%

73%

100%

Chapter One:
The Man Who Would Be King

Tenzing strides ahead of me up the steep cobbled path towards the monastery. Looking upwards at him getting progressively further ahead, I feel frustrated not to be able to match his pace; my body is used to getting far more oxygen than is available in the thin air up here. I have to squint as I look upwards at him. The cloudless and saturated blue sky behind him is strangely ethereal. Despite the cold, the rising sun warms us, reflecting off the whitewashed buildings.

In many parts of the world I get introduced to people calling themselves Johnny (or its local equivalent), who obviously have a real name but choose to keep it secret. I guess they have found it's too hard for foreigners to pronounce or remember. But Tenzing really is called Tenzing, a popular name not just in Nepal but also here on the Tibetan Plateau. There is something about him that I put down to a military bearing and appearance, but I haven't asked him about his background. I suspect he has a particular set of skills that I hope won't be needed during our time together. Nonethless it's reassuring to know that he's probably trained and prepared for any eventuality. Relaxed but confident, Tenzing is in many ways the perfect travel companion. His best asset is his smile. He smiles brightly when he speaks to anyone, and seems to have friends absolutely everywhere. He is proof that positive body language and politeness can get you just about anything you want.

Every few minutes he turns back to me and asks if I want to stop for a break, but I'm stubborn and determined to keep going. Unacclimatised to the altitude as I am, this small hill is proving a significant challenge to my feeble legs and lungs. Pilgrims and kids stride effortlessly past me, spinning huge brass prayer wheels as we make our way towards the entrance to the main courtyard. Spotting a bench on a rocky outcrop I have to stop – not only due to the urgent demands of my body, but also because I need time for my senses to take in the emerging scene in front of me. Suntanned monks in their dark haematite-coloured robes are directing visitors as they enter the monastery.

Pilgrims wave their arms in a mad fashion and whirl about at the bottom of the big stone steps. Some even crawl forwards on their bellies. Hypnotic sounds of bells ringing and Tibetan horns. Clouds of incense mixed with the scent of local flowers and juniper berries. Pinch myself hard. Have I arrived onto the film set of one of my favourite Kipling films, 'The Man Who Would be King'?

Once inside the outer walls, we walk together up the main path, where a long line of people, mainly women and children, are waiting. Many of the younger kids are crying and screaming, while the older ones just look miserable. This is very unusual in Tibet. Tenzing puts his smile on and leans over a little fence to speak to a monk at the entrance to the nondescript stone building. Not sure what to do, I stand at a respectable distance behind the line. Without explanation Tenzing returns and gestures for me to follow him through the crowd, whereupon another monk appears and opens a small side door that I hadn't noticed until then. The door is quickly shut behind us before the crowd notice us, leaving us alone and in the dark. As my eyes adjust, Tenzing explains that the monks here hold blessings for ill children in the afternoons. Our arrival has coincided with the Tibetan equivalent of a long wait at accident and emergency.

But we are not here for a blessing, and I don't yet know the purpose of our visit. I have a suspicion that we're now inside a building that we probably shouldn't be in. Around us lie dusty wooden cabinets and cupboards on a rough stone floor. Trickles of light penetrate through the cracks between the wooden planks of the heavy shutters covering the windows, and once Tenzing has found the switch, a solitary light bulb glows dimly above us.

I'm about to step forwards, but there is something unusual about the floor. Tenzing's arm holds me back and steadies me. I begin to make out strange shapes. In front of me on the ground is a complex painting made of many coloured sands: a mandala. It's about 3 metres square with incredible detail. The purpose of our visit here is for my introductory lesson from Tenzing in the symbolism of Tibetan Buddhism, and he explains to me how meditative monks have constructed this intricate design to represent the transient nature of material life. You have to concentrate hard and somehow imagine the shapes of the mandala inside yourself. The circles become a never-ending life, and proof thateverything is connected. I stare at the pattern until I'm a bit cross-eyed and dizzy. Unused to the practice of meditation, I fail to reach enlightenment today. I shall have to return to complete my spiritual journey another time. With my first lesson over, I'm free to examine the objects in the cabinets nearby, while Tenzing goes into a passageway to look for the way through into the next room. It's strangely peaceful to be almost alone in here whilst still being able to hear the commotion outside.

When Tenzing returns he looks slightly concerned. This wouldn't mean anything to you unless you knew that normally his facial expression is one of beaming happiness, so even looking normal is a sign that something might be wrong. The trouble is that the doors in front of us and behind us are both locked shut. I have no fear, though. After all, I'm with a man who I suspect has been trained to break out of places more secure than this. He scans the room, tries a few other doors, and then jumps up to see if he can get to a little window. They are all securely locked. He pushes and adjusts the position of a couple of the cabinets, looking for a hidden doorway. I can't help but smile despite our circumstances. I'm back in one of my favourite childhood movies…all I need is a bull whip and the right hat. But dark thoughts cross my oxygen-starved mind. I hope Tenzing has a plan, otherwise a hundred years from now a monk might open the door and discover a couple of skeletons next to the mandala. Tenzing starts to bang on the little door, and I join in, as much for moral support as for the extra noise. But with the cacophony outside, no one can hear us.

Chapter Two:

The Edinburgh Explorers Club

South Learmont Gardens is a quiet Edinburgh crescent with attractive Georgian architecture. There is nothing particularly Scottish about it: you could mistake the road and its buildings for the centre of another city of the period, like Bath or Bristol. Idling along the wide pavement I pass elegant town houses, now mainly converted into expensive flats, embassies and boutique hotels. Above the front steps of number 13 is a red awning, and a well-manicured planter sits either side of the front door. A little brass plaque next to the bell push says 'Channings Hotel'. Climbing the stairs and walking past the reception area, I turn left into one of the front rooms. It was the sort of room that the management of the hotel didn't expect you to linger in, but even so they had furnished it with a pair of big chairs and a table with a chessboard. At one time it would have been the parlour of the house next door, but at Channings it was just a room to pass through on the way to the restaurant or your bedroom. My adventure mentor, Keith Parsons, was already there and was busy making notes, his reading glasses perched on the end of his nose. He has drawn a complex looking flowchart, but as I can't read upside down I don't yet know what his new big idea might be. On the table sits the ceremonial and rather battered biscuit tin in which we store the maps and plans of the Edinburgh Explorers Club. Anyone can join our club, but as we haven't told anyone else about it there are currently just two members. Tea arrives in due course and we chat over possible plans, every now and then disturbed by guests looking for directions to the lift. They probably wondered, unaware of the history of the room, why we were sitting here. But we knew. The original house we were in had been the home of Sir Ernest Henry Shackleton between 1904 and 1907. Surely there couldn't be a more inspirational place to plan my adventures than the very parlour room where Sir Ernest would have sat, reading the papers and making arrangements for his next polar expedition.

History suggests, however, that Shackleton's time in Scotland was not the greatest period of his life. Having been rejected as a full-time officer by the

Royal Navy, failing to win a seat as member of parliament in the 1906 general election, and also investing in a doomed business venture involving the transport of Russian troops from the Far East, he bounced back, taking on a job as president of the Scottish Geographical Society. He lived in Edinburgh until he set off on the Nimrod Expedition to find the magnetic south pole. Having met his grand-daughter at the Royal Geographical Society in London, Keith and I were bitten by the Shackleton bug, and spent much time reading and researching his expeditions. Our hobby took us to shipyards, graveyards and buildings across the country. Although Shackleton was very much a public figure in his own lifetime, he was almost forgotten during much of the 20th century and it is only in more recent times that he has begun to be admired as the inspirational leader most regard him as today.

The meeting of the Edinburgh Explorers Club today was a short one, as I had agreed to give a talk to a few people about my travels in Siberia. Tea and biscuits consumed, Keith and I headed to a little meeting room across the hall. We liked this room as it actually contained a few Shackleton artefacts: letters, a bottle of scotch, and early photographs, almost hidden in a glass-fronted cabinet behind the door. My presentation was a bit rushed, and the projector bulb was so dark that I had to describe some of my pictures, but the audience seemed to find my new career as a long-range rail adventurer interesting enough to ask lots of questions. I don't have a lot in common with Sir Ernest, except that he too had to fund his exploration with lecture tours, and we have both travelled to places that were extremely cold. But he got to talk about cute penguins and ships, and I get to talk about rabid dogs and trains.

After the talk we all moved into the bar, where further questions came thick and fast. And then the question that always gets asked: 'Where to next?' The answer was slightly complicated, so I unfolded a map and spread it out on the bar top. It had various routes marked in different inks, and annotations scribbled all along the lines that extended from Europe to Asia. I pointed out the various borders, no-go zones and visa complications of each of the coloured lines. Everyone loves an aspiring adventurer with a map; it somehow gives your plans more respectability. The answer was yet to be decided. After a few pints of Deuchars my audience thinned out, so Keith and I made plans for a late-night curry with Mark Hudson, another close supporter of my adventures. I don't know how many poppadums are the correct adult human portion, but that night we consumed several large piles of them whilst I explained my options in more detail, waiting for some reaction. Mark, normally the 'that doesn't sound very safe' kind of person, is at times touchingly concerned for my personal wellbeing. On the other hand, Keith is the 'what are you waiting for' friend, more interested in bigger and badder adventures, even ones that feel out of my reach. Together they make a well-balanced double act of different schools of thought. I am inspired by the energy of others, and I also use moments like this to make myself commit to doing things that are outside my comfort zone. Once I've said I'm going to do it, there's no going back – it's a binding contract with myself. So that evening, by the time the chicken madras arrived I felt I was ready to commit to a plan, but there seemed to be two competing routes: one was to take the train from Beijing to Lhasa, only possible since 2006, and the other to explore the less well known Trans-Manchurian route through Siberia, the long way round: by-passing Mongolia, going directly into China's north-eastern region, Manchuria, and then down to Beijing. High on the endorphin rush of weapons-grade curry, I realised that there was nothing to stop me combining the two. To travel on the longest and then the highest railways in the world together, as one grand adventure. I would take the train from Edinburgh to Lhasa.

Back then, in that beer-and-chilli-fuelled moment, it all seemed very simple.

Chapter Three:
The Manchurian Candidate

Back at my desk the next day I made some calls to people I knew and trusted, to check the feasibility of the idea. I wanted to know if it could become a real plan. My notes were hand written on cards laid out in order of priority, top to bottom, left to right. When I'd worked in a large company, over time I had learnt the value of a well-organised desk. I used to have one until facilities management introduced the concept of hot desking, and then I lost my personal space and, along with it, its good order. Desks became transitory and unloved spaces where only boring things happened. Nothing interesting could be found on them, just the rubbish of the previous user.

But now, determined to have a place of inspiration in my new life as a rail adventurer,

I had created a desk space to help me deliver my plans. Only pens of the same type were allowed in the same pot; notebooks were colour coded; and I wrote in each book in different coloured inks to remind me where I was. Next to my banker's lamp was a small collection of artefacts and icons to help inspire me. These included a piece of wood from the hull of Sir Francis Chichester's round-the-world yacht Gypsy Moth V, a late uncle's WW2 commando dagger, an ornate metal and glass Russian Railways teacup, and a framed cartoon I had been given that depicted someone who looked rather like me (with an unusually large head) arriving at the fireside cooking spot of a tribe of happy cannibals. The caption underneath read 'Unwittingly, Matthew stepped out of the jungle and into headhunter folklore forever'. It always made me smile. My desk was the place where I needed to turn those curry-fuelled ideas into reality.

Confirmation that the journey was actually going to be possible came a day or two later when the company that fixes my visas had spoken to their contact in Beijing. I had become quite used to the red tape of getting visas and tickets for long train journeys, but this new adventure was at times an exercise in lateral thought. To visit Tibet you needed a special permit, which would only be issued if you had an approved guide from the government and approved accommodation. There were several grades of permit, ranging from travel just on the Tibetan Plateau through to one for climbing Mount Everest. But there was a snag. You couldn't get this permit without a visa first, but if you applied for a tourist visa for China and said you were going to travel to Tibet it would apparently be refused. This was a Catch 22.

The work-around recommendation was a strange one, but it seemed to be the only solution: apply for a Chinese visa with simpler travel plans and then, once it had been issued, change the plans and apply for the Tibet permit. But the application needed to include confirmed hotel bookings, and a detailed travel itinerary, so I worked on a touristic trip around the sights of China and made some reservations. The application went off to the embassy in London – but I couldn't wait for the outcome of this process, as I needed to ensure I was able to get a reservation made on other trains, most importantly the Trans-Manchurian that would take me from Moscow to Beijing the long way around. Instead of crossing Mongolia and the Gobi Desert as in my first Trans-Siberian adventure, I would head further eastwards in Siberia, and then south into Manchuria, to Harbin, and down through the rustbelt of the provinces of north-eastern China. If I was refused a Tibet permit I would need a Plan B once I reached Beijing. For the time being I put Plan B to the back of my mind.

In between long bouts of form filling I read quite a lot, trying to get a feel for the places that I would be visiting. Books about conflict in Manchuria, books about tackling the Himalayas from the Chinese side, and climbing books about the potentially fatal problems at high altitude. They were a luxury that I didn't have room to carry, so I photocopied vital pages and made copious notes in the style of school exam revision. Not only were the books too big and heavy, but they would probably also get me in trouble if spotted by customs officials. My understanding was that any book that shows Tibet as a country on a map is prohibited in China, along with any pictures of the current (14th) Dalai Lama.

Emails started to arrive from my visa agents in London and Moscow, most of them encouraging. I updated the cards on my desk and moved them around, and at the same time as each of the arrangements were confirmed I changed the colours of relevant cells to green on my spreadsheet. Then the day finally arrived when I heard that I had a Chinese tourist visa in my passport. This was great news. I used to fret about the amount of detail required for a successful Russian visa application, but I think on balance they are easier to complete than the Chinese equivalent, which requires lots of backup documentation. I was now able to cancel all the dummy reservations, and my agent in London passed the red tape baton over to an officially approved Chinese travel agent who would apply for the permit allowing travel on the Tibetan Plateau. The rules seemed straightforward: once you had a visa, a guide and ground arrangements it was in the bag. As long, that is, as your plans didn't clash with any significant religious dates in the Chinese calendar, when without warning no permits would be issued to foreigners. I wondered if they were conducting background checks on me.

I found a zipped ring binder to store all the paperwork that I would need to travel with. It grew comfortingly thick with reservations and official documents. When real tickets s tarted to arrive through my letterbox, it was a sure sign it wasn't long until blast-off. Getting a ticket on the Trans-Mongolian and Trans-Siberian train can be tricky if you leave it too late, but I suspected there was no problem travelling through Manchuria, especially in the middle of winter – there would be few reasons for people to punish themselves with this route rather than the easier alternatives. I photocopied each ticket and also scanned them, as a backup. I attached these to an email that I would be able to access wherever I was in the world as long as it had the internet. The last thing to arrive back on my desk was my scruffy-looking passport. I read somewhere that well used passports were actually better than clean ones. Officials generally assume that a lived-in travel document was less likely to be a fake. On this basis I should be just fine. The red tape was complete.

Next I needed to decide what to take on this rail journey and, just as importantly, what to pack it into. Having nearly crippled myself with a giant-size duffel bag in 2014, for my next journey I'd then purchased a wheeled bag big enough for me to climb into. My resolve this time was to travel much lighter, and to find a bag with soft sides, so that I could wedge it into the varying sizes of the luggage spaces on sleeper trains. I have read about the supposed dimensions of the storage spaces under the seats on different trains, but in my experience no two trains are ever alike. In the end I found a bag I liked in my local branch of a department store that never likes to be knowingly undersold. It had a pair of rugged wheels, lots of zips and big straps around the outside to compress the contents. On the top was an extending handle, and I worked out that I could use this to anchor a second, smaller bag. It didn't make me feel very much like an explorer, but at least I had something that I knew would be suited to my needs.

The new bag filled fast with all the usual practical items. First aid kit, thermos flask, winter boots, camera gear, plugs, adapters, batteries, tools, rope and tape. But it would be mad to head off without a jar of Marmite, a bag of jelly babies, some Coleman's mustard powder, and of course my trusty portable espresso machine. The only snag was I wasn't sure where my clothes would go. But after a few attempts, somehow it all squashed in. With my legs holding the bag down I heaved on a couple of compression straps until it looked like I might be carrying less than I actually was.

The spreadsheet for my journey, now complete with massive amounts of detail coloured mostly in green, was large enough to look like it might relate to the movement of an army brigade to a distant battlefield. But my diary was much simpler. Prior to my departure date, other than the dates for a few work meetings, there was just a day in December that said 'Tibet' and a long grey line spanning several weeks.

My favourite armchair in Channings Hotel was a good place to read and further research my journeys. I got seriously inspired there; perhaps the spirit of Sir Ernest was rubbing off on me. I began to feel that anything might be possible. The afternoons flew by with several pots of Assam tea and a pile of books about the great railways of the world and the history of Tibet. Once you're out on the rails of the legendary Trans-Siberian, as you sit in a comfy modern climate-controlled carriage it's all too easy to forget about the history of its construction. You take it for granted. But it wasn't always that easy. The 9289-kilometre line from Moscow to Vladivostok was finished in 1890. More than 60,000 men had laboured on it under the supervision of Tsar Nicholas II, creating one continuous set of tracks across the vast expanse of Siberia. Then millions of migrants headed east on the line, opening the region up to agriculture and industry. Today it is still far cheaper to deliver a container from China to western Europe by train than it is by ship. Most people use the words 'Trans-Siberian' to mean any of the major routes – the original line to Vladivostok, the Trans-Manchurian to Beijing that opened in 1902, and the Trans-Mongolian to Beijing that was not finished until 1961. It is now actually possible to travel on a single train from Kiev to Vladivostok, a journey of over 11,000 kilometres – the longest continuous rail service in the world.

Other than its vast size and beauty, Siberia is perhaps best known for its brutal climate. But as a surprise to the unprepared, the summer can be quite hot, and the temperature variation between the seasonal highs and lows can range by over 100°C. The southern plains familiar to Trans-Siberian rail travellers have a relatively mild continental climate, with a longer, warmer summer than other parts of the region. Yet in winter at Irkutsk, near Lake Baikal, the average daytime January temperature is -20°C – but this can drop to -50°C. If you like your weather extreme, to the north and east is of Irkutsk lies the 'pole of cold', and at its heart a place called Oymyakon, best known for its record-breaking temperatures. Not for the climatic faint hearted, it ranges from +35°C in July to -67°C in January.

Fortunately, Russian Railways (RZD) have plenty of experience of operating in this climate. Their ability to run scheduled services across the continent in almost any weather is impressive to people like me who come from a country where leaves on the line or the wrong sort of snow are enough to cause widespread delays and cancellations. On board these trains, carriages are heated to close to 30°C inside, powered by both electricity and a coal-fired boiler. In winter it is quite normal to have a temperature difference of more than 60°C between your sleeping compartment and the other side of the thin metallic skin that separates you from the outside world.

But even the achievements of Russian Railways in this environment have been eclipsed. At the time of writing, the newest engineering marvel of the railway world is the Qinghai–Tibet railway, which opened in 2006. At just under 2000 kilometres long, it manages to cross the mountains and permafrost of the Tibetan Plateau to reach Lhasa. At times more than 5000 metres above sea level, it has managed to overcome several major construction challenges. No less than 675 bridges have been built, and many tunnels at high altitude, one over 20 kilometres long. One of the biggest challenges to overcome was that the railway line has to sit on a semi-frozen layer that becomes unstable in the summer months. This crust would turn into mud beneath the trains were it not for the ammonia heat exchangers that have been drilled into the ground to keep it cool. Not only that, but long stretches of the rails run on bridges lifting the trains off the ground altogether, protecting the lines from heave and movement in the top layer. No wonder it took almost 22 years to build.

Then there is the train itself. It is no ordinary set of locomotive and carriages, but a purpose-built high-altitude trainset. Twin locomotives haul the carriages, which have shielded windows to protect their passengers from the extra-harmful radiation of the sun at altitude. Inside the air is enriched with oxygen to emulate a lower altitude and reduce the potential for altitude sickness. The compartment doors are semi-sealed to hold the air in and minimise pressure changes within the carriage. Underneath the train there is extra shielding to prevent damage from the ice and sand.

I make a few notes in my little book. 'Effects of altitude?', 'Drugs?' and 'Sun cream'. Travel to high altitude can be dangerous – but surely not in a train enriched with oxygen? It turns out that many get ill from the effects of the train's rapid climb to over 5000 metres. In contrast, mountain climbers ascend slowly, often returning to rest at lower altitude each night. Gradual gain in height means better acclimatisation. I did some climbs a few years ago and remember how I felt on the summit of Kilimanjaro. Gulping down mouthfuls of air, I progressed pitifully slowly – but I did continue to progress; many of those who had ascended more rapidly dropped out completely well before reaching the summit. The air pressure at the top is only about 40% of what it is at sea level, so the effective amount of oxygen in the thin air is much less. No wonder I was gulping air; I was having to breathe deeply to get perhaps half of what my lungs were used to. My eyes saw only saturated colours as the sun rose over Mount Kenya. I even had momentary out-of-body hallucinations as we reached the summit. But I made it.

So, how would this work out on a train? On this journey the 21% oxygen in the air at sea level would drop to around 11% effective oxygen at the Tanggula Pass on the Tibetan Plateau, around half what I was used to.

Many books have been written for mountain-eers about the symptoms and treatment of altitude-related conditions. Most of the attention is understandably around acute mountain sickness, AMS. It ranges from a mild headache to something that can kill you though the conditions of high-altitude cerebral oedema (fluid around the brain) or high-altitude pulmonary oedema (fluid around the lungs). You might think that these conditions would only affect climbers on Mount Everest, but symptoms can kick in as low as 3000 metres. The way climbers manage to minimise the risk of getting AMS is to ascend slowly, take rest days, go back downhill to sleep at lower altitudes, and ascend no more than around 500 metres per day. Supplemental oxygen is a treatment, but not a solution; if you have acute AMS you need to get down, and fast. But on a train what do you do? There is no way of slowing the climb, and the ascent was going to be 5000 metres in a little over 48 hours.

Fortunately, there are several solutions to reduce risk and the effects of altitude sickness to the high-altitude rail adventurer. Oxygen was going to be available on the train, both generally as it was pumped into the carriages, and a 100% supply from your own bottle if you became unwell. Hydration was of course also easy – just drink lots of tea. By not physically exerting yourself, the chances were also reduced; after all, on the train there's no need to climb. Then there were the drugs: paracetemol or ibruprofen for general headaches, and diamox to minimise the symptoms, headaches and nausea. Mountain guides often disagree about the use of diamox (also known as acetazolamide), as it hides the symptoms of the conditions which could become life-threatening if not dealt with by descent. But for dealing with the symptoms it is highly effective.

So now I had to spend some time learning about the effects of altitude on the body. I read through several articles, noting things to expect like increased frequency of urination and a condition known as periodic breathing, which becomes common at 5000 metres. Because your body is breathing hard and deeply to suck in the air, it is also getting rid of carbon dioxide more efficiently than normal. It's actually getting rid of CO_2 that drives the normal pattern of breathing. But with much less CO_2 to get rid of, your body can stop breathing until it senses a need for more oxygen. This leads to a big gasp. Also, it can mean you wake up in the night feeling like you have stopped breathing. That is because for a very short period you have stopped breathing. In general, people moving to high altitude get poor sleep, and a couple of sources recommended using a sedative like temazapam. That sounded like a step too far me. Not only would

I be comatose in the event of a situation arising, but drugs containing morphine or even codeine were a no go in the Russian Federation.

I started to read up on the effects of diet and altitude, too. I knew that even monks who were vegetarian often ate meat at altitude in order to get appropriate nutrition. But my medical dictionary suggested that carbohydrates were going to be better for me than protein at altitude – something to do with being easier to convert them into energy. It was sounding like noodles and sweet tea would be the mainstays of my meals on the plateau.

My discovery that the train was equipped with ultra violet (UV) protected windows also got me thinking about what the sun might be capable of doing to my skin. For every 300 metres you gain in height, the UV radiation becomes on average 4% stronger. So at 5000 metres, UV is 66% stronger than at sea level. Packing note to self: big hat.

'Earth to Matthew!' Keith Parsons had arrived without my even noticing, and was playing with the chess pieces on the table between us. It was time for our weekly mentoring session; helpful questioning of my plans and a gentle stretching of my goals. 'More tea?' he asked, putting his glasses on and getting out his notebook and a pad of post-it notes.

Time always seems to slow down as a new adventure approaches, and I tend to get apprehensive about what I'm about to do. My mind becomes plagued with uncertainties, and also the big questions: Why am I doing this? What will I gain from it? Will the world continue to turn whilst I'm away? I try to counter this by reminding myself that once I set off I usually normalise life on the rails in a matter of days, and after a week or two I'm simply thriving on living each day at a time, with little concern for the past or the future. The day-to-day excitement of new experiences really are like a drug. I wish they could prescribe that degree of happiness and fulfilment on the NHS.

The scheduled day of my departure was fast approaching and I felt that I was in no man's land. No longer a normal person with a normal job and a normal life – but not yet an adventurer, either. Kicking my heels, all I had left to do was recheck my paperwork and stare at the bag in the corner. I dared not play with it for fear I wouldn't be able to get everything back into it again. I was feeling pretty pleased to leave behind my life in this suburban world. I needed to get on with this.

Chapter Four:
As if by Magic, the Shopkeeper Appeared

However early I get up on the morning of a new adventure, there never seems to be enough time to prepare for final departure. This is mainly due to my need to recheck six times that I have actually turned the gas off and locked the back door. But before I get the urge to check the back door a seventh time, I have a 'Mr Benn' moment. Mr Benn was a 1970s children's cartoon about a seemingly ordinary, smartly suited chap who regularly visited his local fancy dress shop. Each time he entered the shop, as if by magic the shopkeeper appeared and suggested he tries on a particular outfit. Then, when Mr Benn left the back of changing room he wasn't in the shop any more, but transported to a new and unfamiliar place,where he had become a cowboy, a spaceman, a caveman, a pirate, a gladiator. But every adventure has to come to an end, and he found himself back in the shop. Once he had changed back into his suit, he walked back to his home in Festive Road.

But on the way home he usually found a small memento of his latest adventure in his pocket, as if to prove that it hadn't been a dream – it had really happened. And now, pulling on my thick quilted jacket, my hands slip into the comfort of the deep pockets, and there it is. I fish out my lucky Russian Railways pocket watch on its chain, ready to provide me with Moscow time as I cross Siberia. I feel comforted by it, as it reminds me that I have really done this before, and everything's going to be just fine. I might not be a spaceman or a pirate, but once again I am definitely a long-range rail adventurer. So I set off in excitement and anticipation.

Edinburgh is a beautiful city on a bright day, but quite moody when the sun isn't shining. The speed at which it changes from one to the other surprises visitors who are not equipped with suitable clothing. Today, Friday 11 December 2015, the weather is miserable, so I'm glad of my jacket, but making up for this are the bright Christmas lights on the big wheel that has been erected on Princes Street near the Balmoral Hotel. It gives the city an almost fairytale quality. Once down inside Waverley Station, I perch on a bench seat in the ticket hall and wait patiently for my train. The bench is made of bare metal, which quickly chills my flesh; I imagine this is a design feature to avoid people dwelling too long. I like to arrive in good time for trains, hating a last-minute dash: time to find tickets, buy a paper, and get a cup of reasonable coffee to take onto the train (where the coffee can be quite unreasonable). It's my standard operating procedure for catching a train. Anyway, dashing is out of the question today as I'm carrying far too much gear.

Around me today are huddles of fellow travellers, each getting ready to set off on their very own rail adventure. Places I have never visited appear on the departures board. Services to Tweedbank, Helensburgh and Glenrothes are all departing shortly, but the 11.18 to Cowdenbeath has been cancelled. I don't even know where Cowdenbeath is. Why am I so obsessed with taking trains to Lhasa, Guangzhou and Hong Kong when I haven't yet visited all the places in my own country? They sound exotic enough in their own right, and no visas or permits are needed to visit them. I make a mental note to plan some more micro-adventures on my return.

Leaving lots of time for the walk to platform 9, I peel myself off the bench and assemble my bags, ready for their first test of manoeuvrability in a real train environment. Changing direction requires a bit of skill that I don't yet have, but all goes smoothly until I discover that the escalator up to the footbridge is out of use. Taking a deep breath, I lift my bags in both hands and start my ascent of the wide Victorian staircase. About halfway up, my horizon is blocked by a rather stout railway official. 'You're on the wrong side,' he barks at me. I put my bags down on the stairs in case my arms fall off, and consider this for a moment. What he means is that there is a sign saying go up on one side of the stairs, and down on the other, obviously meant for rush hours. But at this moment we're the only people there. I look down at my bags and then at him with a polite smile before continuing my climb as the only passenger on the staircase. 'I've got you marked, pal, we'll see about that!' he shouts at my back. I decide there's nothing I can say that would improve his outlook on life and I keep going. I'm not sure what he has in mind that he's going to see about. Have I broken the law? Would the police be called to deal with a subversive passenger? It saddens me that there are still people like that working in the rail industry, but once I reach the platform I give myself a mental pat on the back for not rising to it. Better that it happens to me than to a tourist on their first trip to Scotland. In many countries I'm sure that the station staff would have even helped me carry my bags, but sadly not here, not this time. I have often imagined that the funniest thing ever would be a fly-on-the-wall documentary on a job exchange between railway employees in Britain and Japan. The visiting Brits would learn about bowing politely to customers, wearing white gloves, litter picking and courteously escorting passengers to the right part of the platform. I'm not so sure what the Japanese would learn from our own rail network.

Most of my experiences of catching a train from Waverley Station were on busy commuter trains in that deep darkness before dawn, often on the way to business meetings about mostly inconsequential things a long way away. Longing to get an extra few minutes of sleep, I would dose fitfully until someone woke me with a microwaved bacon roll and a cup of stewed tea. But now, at this time of day, things were rather more civilised. I was first onto the ageing but comfortable first-class carriage, and loaded my bag onto the empty luggage rack at the far end. The train today was a class 91, the InterCity 225 that had been built to replace the original 125s in the 1980s. Except that they didn't, and so 40 years later both classes were still running up and down the East Coast mainline.

As a small boy I aspired to own the Hornby InterCity 125 train set for my growing OO gauge model railway, but sadly it never appeared under our Christmas tree, and it was well beyond the price of my pocket money, which was 10p a week, not linked to inflation or my age but on a fixed 1p per year increase. Instead I was blessed with an Action Man parachutist (without the eagle eyes), and industrial quantities of Meccano.

Today, first class is filling up with couples and small groups of friends heading off on week-end breaks. They don't seem to have many cares in the world. I keep an eye out for the angry railway worker on the platform in case he tries to boot me out of first class, but am relying on the fact that he won't know which carriage I'm in. A brief announcement from the guard that I can't understand, and we slowly pull out of the station on the southbound line, through the Calton tunnel in the direction of Dunbar.

My adventure is at last under way. I sip fizzy water whilst trying to think of something that I might have forgotten to pack. The best I can come up with is that I have forgotten my beard trimmer. I take this as a good sign that I have probably brought all the essentials in my overstuffed bag. As we whizz past a sign saying 'Edinburgh 50 miles' I figure out that I have a mere 12,461 miles (20,054 kilometres) to cover to Kowloon Hung Hom, the railway terminus for Hong Kong, my final destination.

The food on board is pretty reasonable. Although nearly all British trains now travel without a proper restaurant carriage, the staff still manage to heat and serve tasty food from a little galley kitchen. I opt for the beef curry, which tricks my brain into thinking that I might actually be on board the International Express from Bangkok to Penang. I'm imagining palm trees, warm winds and the smell of freshly ground spices – until I'm brought back to reality by urgently applied squeaking brakes as we come to an unplanned halt outside Berwick-upon-Tweed. Surely, only in the United Kingdom would the guard announce over the public address system of a passenger train: 'The PA is not working in all the carriages on today's service. I would like to apologise if you can't hear this.'

I'm a great believer in a Buddhist approach to rail adventure. In this spiritual code you never ask how long you might be delayed somewhere, but learn instead just to savour the moment and enjoy the extra time in an unexpected place. You never get angry about what might have gone wrong, but instead focus on what's good. You smile at other passengers and ignore any social shortcomings. So this delay is a useful test that my zen is in order. It turns out that another southbound train has broken down in front of us, and so the northbound line is going to be used to let trains pass in both directions, in turn. I sit back and read a few pages of 'Seven Years in Tibet'. There's no hurry today; no connections to miss.

After standing still for over an hour, at last we creep past the crippled train on the other line; its occupants look tired and dejected, and I wonder how long it will be until they are rescued. As we build up speed again the items on my little table vibrate towards the edges in all directions; the driver seems to be making up as much time as possible. When we pass trains in the other direction, the shock wave of the carriages passing closely past at a combined speed of over 200 miles per hour makes my teacup jump in the air. By the time we reach the outskirts of Newcastle, the light is fading outside, and houses are brightly lit with more Christmas lights than you would imagine possible. Their occupants are presumably all out working overtime to fund their increased electricity bills.

I have yet to finally decide if I like Newcastle station or not. It can be pretty bleak in winter, with little space to shelter from an icy wind that blows through the open ends. The locals don't mind of course, as they wear t-shirts and miniskirts whatever the weather, and that's just the men. Non-Geordies, being mere mortals, have to shelter in the Centurion Bar until it's time to depart. But the weather's no problem for me today as I'm dressed for Siberia. Taking my time to haul my bags at a sustainable pace, I cross the single footbridge and bump them down the steps that lead onto the main concourse. I'm greeted here by the strange but somehow familiar smell of electrified trackside debris and warmed-up Cornish pasties.

A night out with a couple of old friends gives me a boost of positivity and Christmas cheer, and I eventually wake in an unfamiliar hotel bed the next morning, smelling of kebab. Whilst I have been dreaming of strange rail-based experiences, a cold front has arrived from the east, and it's snowing outside. Not any old snow, but that inescapable wet snow that saturates everything it touches.

I spend the day dodging snow showers until it's time to get myself down to North Shields to board my ship, the King Seaways, bound for Ijmuiden. I've been on this boat before. It offers a tantalising flavour of what life on board the Titanic might have been like, as it employs class segregation: Commodore Class passengers like me have a key to a private deck with our own lounge. I have nothing against the partygoers who are on a mini-cruise – read 'booze cruise' – but I welcome the isolation from the disco and the chance to get some sleep.

Taking a stroll around the lower deck, I can make out South Shields in the gloom to starboard:

my final view of England, and a moment to say goodbye before we adjust our course to cross the North Sea. I've always loved travelling by ship. The excitement of a whole community with nothing to do but relax. Plenty of public places to socialise in, and a cabin to hide in when you want some privacy. No one's dressing for dinner on the King Seaways, but it still provides an allure of sophistication for its passengers: a casino, a cinema, a duty-free store and a choice of several bars and restaurants. As the evening progresses it becomes a bit wild at sea, and doors slam shut in the gusts as the boat rolls. Retiring to my cabin, I run through my schedule for the next couple of days before turning in for the night.

I don't think I've ever actually had breakfast in bed in a hotel. If I know that breakfast is coming I get up well before its arrival, get dressed and make the bed before anyone knocks on my door. So now, by the time there's a discreet double tap on my cabin door and a friendly Filipino crew member delivers my breakfast tray, I've almost packed my bags. I munch on a strange combination of cheese, salami, apricots and a jam roll whilst watching the docking procedure from the comfort of my cabin. It's time to leave my cocoon and join the scrum of foot passengers ready for disembarkation. Once through Ijmuiden's immigration post, I board a coach to take me to Amsterdam.

The sun has put in an appearance to welcome us to the city today. The Gothic features of the central station glint and gleam as we approach the dropping-off point across the canal out front. The station has been under major renovation for several years, but it's almost finished now and the scaffolding has finally been removed. My plan is a simple one. Rather than hang around for a night train to take me to Poland, I'm heading on a day train to Berlin, where I am to spend a couple of days before picking up the route to Warsaw, Minsk and Moscow. The week-end Deutsche Bahn (DB) train to Berlin isn't an ultra-modern InterCity Express, but a slightly older train that should get me there in around seven hours. Departure is from platform 1, the only platform in the station with anything much going on. I wait in a funky first-class lounge, revving myself up on dark roasted Dutch espresso. My mood is good; I am, after all, about to get going with some continental rail travel. I mainline a final shot of caffeine and head out onto the platform. Finding your carriage on a long train is very easy in most of northern Europe, as somewhere on the platform there is usually a board with pictures of each train showing the order of the carriages. I think it's called a train composition board. As the train rumbles in, I remember that this station has been built over the inland sea on wooden piles. This sounds mad when you think of the weight of the trains passing through.

My carriage is made up of those rather old-school compartments instead of the more modern open-plan layout. I have been trying to learn a few words of local train lingo for this trip. I know a little bit of railway Russian, but as I have rather neglected my railway German, I'm pleased to be able to practise a few words today. On my zug I'm sitting in a fenster – not an expensive guitar, but a seat by the window. However, the international convention for railway ticketing decrees that tickets are issued in just three languages – Russian, German and Chinese. I don't know why they're not in English, but it keeps me on my toes.

There are just six seats in the compartment. This is an interesting alternative to the anonymity of the open plan. At one time this seating arrangement was the norm in Great Britain – though usually, in those days, with eight seats – and I always marvelled at the way commuters managed to ignore each other at such close quarters. I had an uncle who took the train to London Bridge every day for more than 30 years. He knew the names of each of the five season ticket holders he shared a first-class compartment with – but he would never have talked to them unless something was very wrong. The only occasions when this was permissible would have been war being declared somewhere in the home counties or perhaps after the staff Christmas lunch when a little too much sherry had been consumed.

I hide behind my newspaperand subtly observe my fellow passengers. I'm not sure why I'm doing this, but suspect it's an instinctive reaction to watching 'The Great Escape' every Boxing Day afternoon since 1974. But unlike Gordon Jackson, I have no Homburg hat and home-made overcoat, so I suspect my cover would quickly be blown. It's not long before I make eye contact with a tall and strangely familiar-looking gentleman sitting opposite me. It's Mick Fleetwood. He's really friendly and we talk about a few things to pass the time. Rather strangely, though, he speaks with a Dutch accent, and his wife doesn't seem very rock'n'roll to me. She's far too keen on her knitting.

Day trains have a very different feel from the sleepers that run on the same lines during the night. Day trains give you a few hours in a comfy seat with fellow passengers to talk to, or a good book to read if you don't feel like socialising. Most importantly, though, you get a view of life outside the train that you can't see at night, with the blinds drawn in your berth. Not just the distant landscapes of countryside and medium-range suburbia, but also a closer view of people and their way of life at each station. As we cross from the Netherlands and into Germany, it's hard to notice much difference at first. Then I gradually begin to spot changes to the colours of the road signs, the architectural styles of houses, and little details, like the types of police cars and the jazziness of advertisements. The guard appears at the door of the compartment and asks for our papers. (I need to lose this obsession with films about escaping prisoners in the Second World War. She doesn't say 'papers' – what she actually says is 'fahrkarte', tickets.) Everything in order, she wishes us a pleasant journey in the three languages and leaves us to it.

The next carriage along from ours is the Bordobistro. It doesn't disappoint. A smartly dressed waiter with a large moustache stands behind the tidy bar and takes orders. Given all the modernism surrounding him, you might think that he would do this on a tablet or a clever EPOS device that sends messages directly to the kitchen. But no – he writes them down with a pencil on a beer mat. It's both old-school and charming, and the beermat alludes to the greatest triumph of DB's catering: the bar has real draught Erdinger beer, which is served in improbably tall branded glasses. The glasses are so tall and thin that I can't understand how they don't topple over as we take in the curves, banking around the immovable features of the landscape. But this is Germany. They probably have a special test train where mad scientists fill glasses of foamy beer and experiment with them at different G forces. My order placed, I'm invited to go and sit down; a waiter will bring it to me. I'm only a couple of hundred miles from home, but things are already very different on the rails. The train passes factories and industrial complexes that once made Panzer tanks and armoured cars. Now they manufacture kitchen gadgets and prestige cars for aspirational consumers across the world.

Time flies by, and it doesn't feel very long before we're weaving our way through suburban Berlin. In 2006 the city opened a brand-new station, Berlin Hauptbahnhof, replacing the original building on the same site, which dated back to 1876. The design of today's multi-level station is deeply impressive, especially when arriving at night. The railway line is elevated above the city blocks and enters the station via an illuminated entrance to the upper level. This is the final stop for this service today, and once I have bundled my bags onto the platform I take a moment to go back and check I haven't left anything inside the compartment. When my eyes have adjusted to the simulated daylight inside the station, I try to get my head around how this place works. In the bowels are the platforms for the local mass transit U-Bahn and the S-Bahn trains. Next level up are platforms for regular trains, and on top of this is another deck of platforms, crossing those below at a right angle. This is where most of the eastbound express trains leave from. The place is spotless. It doesn't feel like a train station, more a shopping arcade or entertainment centre. I remember seeing a film based on the true story about a man who lived inside a terminal of Paris Charles de Gaulle airport for 18 years. If you were ever going to be stuck inside a railway station, this would be a good one to choose. If I had to vote for the best railway station in the world, I would almost certainly put this one on my shortlist. It would be there with Shinjuku in Tokyo, Beijing South in China and maybe even St Pancras in London.

But it's time to step outside the railway world. With nearly 700 kilometres under my belt for the day, it's time for a beer. The hotel I have chosen is a short walk away and, too tired to head out for the evening, I park myself at its bar. The staff are quirky, clever, fun and efficient all at the same time. How do Berliners manage to be so hip? My Warsteiner beer is everything it should be. It's perfectly poured into a branded glass, and the foamy top is sliced off with a special spatula. The outside of the glass quickly condensates with the temperature of the precious golden liquid inside.

Chapter Five:
Checkpoint Charlie

I have a couple of days to enjoy the Berliner lifestyle before getting back on the rails. It gives me
some time to pursue two of my favourite hobbies:
drinking beer and finding hidden places from a city's
past. People often mention how much a place has
changed since they last visited. Shanghai has a lot
more skyscrapers, and Birmingham has rebuilt its
Bull Ring – but that's nothing compared to Berlin.
When I first travelled there by train in 1988 it was
a still a city divided by a wall, and West Germany
was surrounded by its eastern neighbour. This
was my first ever cold war experience, travelling
from West Germany nearly 160 kilometres eastwards
through the Soviet Bloc along the corridor to the
'island of freedom'. I was on a trip with a couple
of old school friends, Alan and Dicky (not their
real names). Alan had a father who did something

in the service, and had helped arrange a few things; I'm thinking tinker, tailor, soldier, spy. Our East German carriage was drab, dirty and smelled of cheap cigarettes – a proxy for life back then in the GDDR. Once the train was in the corridor it made no stops, protecting comrades living in the Soviet Bloc from capitalist travellers like us. A soldier with an enormous peaked cap and a strangely sick-looking green shirt woke us in the night and inspected our documents. Our big blue passports back then didn't have any biometric features. Inside mine, my name, handwritten in official black ink, was underneath a black & white photograph to which I bore only a limited resemblance. The soldier stamped a single piece of paper; this was a transit visa, making our presence here legitimate.

In Berlin, we had the opportunity of visiting the soviet sector. I can't remember if Alan carried a diplomatic passport, but from the moment we turned up at Checkpoint Charlie we were under a lot of scrutiny. Everything was x-rayed and carefully examined by hand. Cigarettes were individually inspected for listening devices and hidden cameras. Once cleared, compulsory currency exchanges were made and we were free to walk through the barricade and out onto the streets of East Berlin. Trying to spend our non-exchangeable currency, we ordered lunch in a worker's canteen. But as our food arrived a loud bell rang, chairs scraped on the floor and we were left alone as diners hurried back to work. We ate our sausage and sauerkraut in monk-like silence. On the way back towards the wall I felt that strange sensation that we were being followed. It might sound a bit far-fetched now, but in this period the Stasi were watching everyone.

Before we reached the checkpoint I found a kitchen shop with lots of glassware in the window. We had to spend our money on something, and this looked like the best bet. I found some schnapps glasses which I thought would be a good gift for some-one, not that I knew anyone who drank schnapps. But although the bored and miserable woman behind the counter showed me a glass and let me handle it, she wouldn't let me buy it. In the soviet system, you had to pay for the item you wanted at a different counter with another uninterested woman and then return with a receipt to prove ownership. Transaction complete, I left the shop with my glasses wrapped in a few sheets of freshly printed propaganda. Mr Benn would have been proud of my memento from this adventure.

Today the Checkpoint Charlie I remember from the 1980s is mostly just a tourist trap. It has been reimagined to look like something from the period after WW2, with actors dressed up in American GI uniforms and posing for photos. A Christmas tree adorns the sandbags outside the checkpoint building in the middle of the street. But it's still good to enjoy the sense of place and to remember what a divided city was like. Looking back, it's also rather strange to realise how the U-Bahn trains from West Berlin managed to function, criss-crossing east and west beneath the wall. Back then in the eastern sector, surveillance posts and ghost stations covered in barbed wire offered tantalising glimpses of the east to residents of West Berlin. And if you had been in the city in 1989 during the fall of the wall, you would have been able to examine these places because those underground barricades, untouched since 1961, were also removed. Original advertisements and timetables would have adorned the walls. But no one thought to preserve them, so today there is virtually nothing left of these cold war relics.

Leaving the warmth of the Magdalenenstrasse U-Bahn station, I cross the street and enter a nondescript office building in the back streets of Lichtenberg that the concierge has marked for me with a big cross on a tourist map. The receptionist knows why I'm here and sells me a ticket for 8 Euros. Once I have shown this to the guard I climb up two flights of imposing stairs and enter an office still furnished exactly as it had been in the 1960s: at one end of the room is a big desk with several telephones, and at the other a soft seating area. This was once the office of Erich Meilke, the Minister of State Security for

East Germany. I'm inside the former Stasi headquarters, one of the most repressive intelligence agencies to have ever existed.

I find it hard to imagine a society where secret agents are embedded into every aspect of life, responsible for the suppression of any activity deemed inappropriate by the state. Here, at the height of the Stasi's power, there was one security officer for every 166 people in East Germany, forming the largest secret police force in history. The Stasi building has been well preserved, packed full of photographs and objects from these dark times, still in the context of the original offices vacated in a hurry in late 1989. They say that during the peaceful revolution that year more than a billion sheets of paper were recovered. I wondered if one of those sheets might have been a field report of my activities in East Berlin with Alan and Dicky back in 1987. You can make a request today to find out if there's a file on you. I take an application form from the receptionist, but have yet to submit it. I have a strange foreboding about what might be revealed, and would rather not know.

In the evenings I drink local beer at my local station bar, the Hopbraufinger. They take both their sausages and their beer so seriously that you have to admire the place. I would like to think that I might one day be considered to be a local if I were to visit it every day for a couple of years. It has taken me a long time to realise how much I appreciate the Germanic character: everything is done with careful planning and precision, but they're not afraid to be open and honest and have fun. I rather admire these character traits. I used to scuba dive quite a bit in Asia, and always found German-run dive boats to be the best. Serious dive masters would oversee carefully planned deep dives with military precision, but once out of the ocean they would drink draught beer from a bar on the boat whilst motoring back to port.

To reach the Hopbraufinger on foot from my hotel, all I have to do is cross the square in front of the main station. The problem is that this is also the place where the police allow public protests to take place, and business is brisk. Fleets of police vans arrive without warning and deploy barriers to keep the groups apart. I have no idea what tonight's protest is about, but it's noisy and more than a little intimidating from the sidelines. As a bona fide non-participant, I appeal to a couple of policemen to let me through. They are friendly but firm: I'm not going through the middle of this. Instead I'm directed towards the chanting crowd on one side. How do the police know which group I might belong to? My mission now, should I choose to accept it, is to switch sides without being noticed, so I can make it across the square and into the station. I think about walking backwards, but before I have time to plan any further I find myself in the company of some men with a love of black leather and big beards. Although they look like they might eat small dogs for breakfast, they turn out to be rather polite and, once they realise what I'm trying to do, escort me towards my destination. The expected standard of behaviour here seems to be noisy but thankfully peaceful.

Early the next morning I check out of my hotel. It isn't actually that early, but I feel like I need a lie-in after so much beer and sausage the previous night. Back inside the glass-domed world of the Berlin Hbf, I stop for some coffee before heading upwards to platform 11. Up at the top of the escalator the platform resembles the hop-on point of a rollercoaster ride, but one without a queue. At the end of the platform, the tracks sweep out into thin air and over the top of some nearby buildings. A chilly breeze blows in from the east, so I take refuge behind a vending machine and stuff my hands deep into the pockets of my down jacket to keep warm. The next train to Warsaw is the EC43, and as it approaches it too looks like something from the fairground. The Polish locomotive belonging to PKP, Polish State Railways, is painted bright pink, Pantone reference Barbie. It pulls some traditionally coloured carriages adorned with the words

Berlin Warsawa Express painted on their sides. Calling the train an express for the six-hour ride between the two capitals is perhaps tempting fate.

It isn't a busy train, and once on board carriage 272 I find myself alone in the now familiar six-seat compartment. Seat reservations are pinned to a board outside the sliding door, and there don't seem to be any others in here apart from my own. Spreading out in my comfy fenster, I relax as we navigate our way through the maze of tracks to the east of the city. My order of business is clear. I'm going to treat myself to a 'full Polish', the amazingly good breakfast of perfectly spiced scrambled eggs with sausages that PKP serve on branded bone china plates in their restaurant carriage. Today this is carriage 270, right next door to my home for the day. The only problem with this plan is that carriage 270 isn't next to mine or anywhere else to be seen. When I ask the conductor, he tells me they have forgotten to add it to the train this morning. This sounds rather careless to me, but he says it like it's quite normal. Was this just lost in translation, or has carriage 270 actually been accidentally abandoned somewhere in a shunting yard? Chef might be cooking breakfast unaware that he's going to be alone for the day. But I haven't packed any food for the journey, and I'm hungry. Reflecting on my fate, and guilty of breaking a long-range rail travel rule, I don't even have any water with me.

Sleep comes without me realising how tired I actually am. I awake mid-snore with a jolt as we pull to a halt at Frankfurt (Oder), the Polish border. I continue to doze for a bit, but something feels wrong – it's the sixth sense that wakes solo sailors and gets them up on deck before they hit an iceberg. After half an hour we haven't moved. Out on the platform nothing much is happening, other than a few passengers smoking and waiting for news. Leaving the comfort and warmth of the compartment behind, I hop off to investigate. The conductor is standing next to the locomotive and is busy exchanging texts on her mobile. It could be either her lover or the office; her face is hard to read. She speaks some English, however, but the news isn't brilliant. The train is due a crew change, but for some reason no one has turned up here to take over the train. We could be here for some time, and exactly how long isn't clear.

I don't know quite what comes over me, but in a moment of madness, I consider breaking another cardinal rule of long-distance rail travel: never let a train out of your sight when your luggage is still on board. But I need food, and it can't be far away. I explain my predicament to the conductor, and she thinks about it, which seems to take quite a while considering how long she reckons we might be here. So I finish up by saying,

'You promise you won't leave without me?' She smiles, looks at me with her kind blue eyes and says, 'For sure.'

Running down the ramp to the tunnel between the platforms, I feel the sense of excitement of a schoolboy bunking off a double maths class. In the booking hall I find a small bakery and procure enough ham and cheese rolls to last a couple of days. I also manage to balance a fresh cup of coffee in my other hand before retracing my steps. It's human nature not to want to be stranded, and this is exactly the sort of thing that I frequently have nightmares about. But I decide not to run back; it would end up like one of those children's television shows where the objective of the game is to cross the finish line of the obstacle course with the most water left in a bucket. I've only been gone for ten minutes, and feel I can chance a more leisurely pace back to the train so that I can arrive with both a full cup of coffee and some dignity.

But on reaching the top of the ramp up to my platform I regret this decision, as the train is nowhere to be seen. Bugger. Don't panic, Captain Mainwaring!

Unfortunately, the panic part of my brain is firmly in charge, some sort of caveman wiring. Rational thought is overwhelmed by the mad person in my head. I look up and down the empty platform as though the train might actually still be there but momentarily invisible to me. Trying to read the platform departures board as calmly as possible, I can't make sense of it. My train is missing, apparently lost in the German equivalent of the Bermuda Triangle for railways. There is no sign of the very existence of my train. It has been erased from history.

The station staff man sees me before I see him. He's the sort of chap who carries that plastic baton to wave in the air to let the driver it's okay to depart, and he's had time to work me out as I shuffle over. 'EC43,' I ask him. 'Where is the EC43? Warsaw?' He understands me but pauses before answering, giving me a rather pitying look up and down. Then he waves his baton in the air as if performing a conjuring trick, and points at that very train, still sitting forlornly without its crew on the opposite platform. It has of course always been there and in my haste I have emerged on the wrong one.

We finally get on the move again after a couple of hours. Had I known, I could have enjoyed a proper lunch in a place outside the station, perhaps even with a cheese course. The new conductor spends quite a long time apologising on the public address system, explaining in his native Polish why we're so late. His actual words are wasted on me, but I sense genuine remorse in his tone. In the style of aid workers on the scene at a minor disaster, a young woman wearing a hi-vis waistcoat and carrying several mobile phones arrives at my compartment and issues some emergency rations of water and biscuits. Not just the ubiquitous PKP Prince Polo wafer biscuits, but chocolate, almond and raisin cookies. Things must be really bad.

As the train passes through the frozen agricultural landscape the light outside seems to fade even earlier than usual. An eerie mist obscures distant views, drawing in the premature arrival of night. Lights flicker on in passing settlements and fires burn in their little wooden houses. The fields eventually give way to the outer suburbia of Warsaw. Living next to the railway lines here looks pretty tough: row upon row of small brick lockups with piles of scrap outside, flanked further back by blocks of brutalist flats designed by architects from Moscow. Then there's the underclass: people living in wood and plastic ramshackle tents right next to the embankment and under the bridges. But as we get closer to the city centre these are all obliterated by a world of smooth graffiti-covered concrete.

All the platforms at Warsaw Centralna station have been built underground, creating a brightly lit subterranean world. Above, on the surface, there is just a single huge booking hall. There has been talk about knocking it down for some time, but somehow it lives on as a relic of cold war architecture. Once through its busy passageways and up a long flight of stairs, I drag my bag through the snow and slush of the wide pavements in the direction of my hotel. Were it not for the cheery people, you couldn't make the city look any less welcoming in winter; mostly bombed flat in the Second World War, it's a bleak-looking place. The only architectural cheer comes from the colourful lights of the nearby Palace of Culture, the tallest building in Poland, designed and built by the Soviets in 1955. Some locals call it Stalin's Syringe or the Russian Wedding Cake.

Advertising often gives me the first impression of what it might be like to live in a place that I'm passing through. Here the bus stop hoardings promote strange cuts of meat from the local supermarket, cheap mobile phone deals and brightly coloured clothes from C&A. People on the pavements stay close to the buildings, ducking in and out of the doorways. On the road, lines of obedient drivers in family cars crawl forward through the salty slush.

I can't fit all my bags through the revolving door of the hotel entrance at once. This is clearly a test of my lateral thinking, like the puzzle when you have to work out how to ferry the chicken, the sack of corn and the fox across the river. But I don't want to risk leaving any of my precious cargo behind, so I find a staff entrance round the side of the building. Inside, it would seem the party has already started. Guests are dressed up and enjoying pre-dinner drinks. I fantasise that I might blag an invitation to whatever this party is, but I know I'm not going to make the cut, based on the dress code alone. I head over to the reception desk where a smartly dressed manager is dispensing room keys to impatient businessmen. As I head up to my room on the 19th floor I have time in the lift to reflect on my day. I like it when things don't go to plan. Well, mostly. It tests my zen and stretches my tolerance of not being in control. If you stretch this bit by bit, like a muscle, it learns to cope with bigger problems.

There's time before dinner for a soak in the bath with a panoramic view out over the city. I've always raised my eyebrows when I've seen a telephone in a hotel bathroom – I'm quite happy to make calls from the desk in my bedroom, rather than when I'm in the shower or on the toilet. But tonight, I take a call from my bath. It's Reception, passing on a message that at first neither of us understand. 'The police car will meet you here at 10 am. Mariosh.'

Chapter Six:
Carriage 344

Waking up in a strange bed once again, it takes me a few moments to remember where I am. The room is decorated in a bland and flowery transatlantic hotel style that was popular in the early 1990s; I could be in Washington, Wisconsin or Wolverhampton. Breakfast is hot and voluminous, setting me up for a day on the frozen streets: scrambled eggs, buffet-style overcooked fatty rashers of bacon, and stewed coffee poured by eager waiters from large plastic flasks.

True to his word, Mariosh is there to meet me in the hotel reception at 10 am. The police car is actually a retired police van, repurposed and painted canary yellow. He's going to show me around the Praga, the district across the river, far enough away from the centre of the city to have escaped bombing in the last war. Dressed in the style of a mad professor, he wears little round glasses and carries an attaché case stuffed with pictures of old Praga. Like many young Poles, he's driven and entrepreneurial enough to have set up his own business. He makes his money by guiding people around hidden parts of the city in strange vehicles.

Praga retains markets, courtyard slum buildings and bars that give it a more bohemian feel than central Warsaw. I share Mariosh's police car experience with a Japanese journalist. The three of us must make quite a strange sight on the streets. The markets are piled high with an eclectic mix of typewriters, tools, medals and vintage cameras; I could spend hours looking through piles of this kind of stuff. Lunch is in a local 'milk bar' – a café and social refuge, serving traditional comfort food through a hatch next to the counter. Some of the customers stagger a bit too much. Once we're stuffed full of dumplings and cabbage rolls we squeeze back into the van and head back to the city centre.

The general manager appears at Reception to say goodbye as I am checking out. Rather touchingly she wishes me a safe trip, adding that she will never ever forget me. I could pretend that this was because I'd inspired her with my love of her city, but the truth is rather more embarrassing. Soon after I'd checked in I asked to change rooms owing to a drilling noise from the renovation works on a floor below. Back to Reception, who quickly found me a new room further away from the works. But the sound was just as bad in the new room. I was on the spur of asking to be moved a second time when I deduced that the noise was not actually emanating from the walls of the hotel, but rather from inside my big bag. The drilling sound was actually my battery-powered toothbrush. I did the honourable thing and explained my faux pas to the duty manager when I next passed Reception, and immediately entered hotel guest folklore – I seem to have hit a sweet spot in Polish humour.

Reluctantly leaving behind the comfort and excitement of the buzzing hotel lobby in the early evening, I head over to the main concourse of the station via a number of warm and smelly subterranean passageways. Having been caught out by the lack of catering on the last train, I want to find out more about the D10 Schnellzug (express train) to Moscow. Finally reaching the front of the queue at the information counter, I'm disappointed to discover that no English is spoken here, other than the words 'InterCity Office', as the man gesticulates to the other side of the building. There stands a massive queue of hopeful passengers wanting to get reservations. As I don't actually need a ticket, I feel I could chance drifting to the front just to ask a quick question. With the eyes of the queue burning into my back, I approach the desk and smile at the stressed-out man sitting behind his computer screen nursing a badly chewed ballpoint pen. It turns out he doesn't know about things like restaurant carriages, so he calls his supervisor, who isn't very sure either. It isn't long before the whole office seems to be trying to find an answer to my question, rather than selling tickets to the growing line of travellers. The office manager is horrified to discover that I have managed to derail the queue with such a foolish question and informs me flatly that there will be no on-board catering on this train. With this news I thank the gaggle of staff, and turn and smile at the queue whilst trying to avoid eye contact. I shuffle out of the office to find a supermarket to buy some suitable rations for the next 24 hours.

The D10SZ is a brand-new Russian train that has replaced its sometimes Polish, sometimes Russian, D10 predecessor, and it's in its first week of daily service between Warsaw and Moscow. The only downside of the new arrangement is that it doesn't depart until the early evening, which will mean a late night of red tape on the Belarus border. Rule number 2 in my long-distance rail code is to never to be late for a night train, so I arrive on the platform (called a tor here in Poland) with more than half an hour to spare. Rather impressively, there are friendly multilingual staff to help people find the right place on the platform to stand for their carriage. This is clearly more than a commute, more of a migration, as passengers wait with suitcases and piles of bags. A single light on the front of the locomotive is visible in the tunnel, then the deep rumble of the approaching train. As it passes me I'm rather pleased to discover that it's pulling a set of gleaming carriages painted in the latest RZD corporate colour scheme.

Carriage 344 is located towards the front of the train, and by the time I reach it the provodnitsa has already dismounted. Her name is Lira, and she checks that I am on her manifest before inspecting my ticket. As I climb up into the carriage I'm greeted by that special kind of smell that you find in new things made of metal and plastic; the carriage has recently been delivered fresh from the factory in Austria. The décor is tasteful and calming. My bed for the night is in a four-berth compartment, and it looks like I'm going to be by myself tonight. The only thing that isn't perfect is that I'm right down the end next to the toilets. It's best to get a compartment in the middle of a sleeper train if you can; that way you avoid noise from the outer doors and any aroma from either illicit smokers or the toilets. Being further away from the bogies also means that the ride is often smoother, as the suspension cushions the ride. But it's no hardship being at the end of the carriage, as it feels quite luxurious. Once I have worked out how to put the other three berths away, I sit on my bed and note some of the features of its design: carefully laid-out switches for lighting and air conditioning, modern power points, and locks designed with the care and attention to detail you would expect from the country that now supplies the British Army with its latest polymer-framed handguns.

Lira returns my ticket and, as we pass slowly through the east side of the city, she explains how everything works. I always like to make a close target recce of the rest of the carriage before settling in, and today I hit the jackpot with an amazing discovery. What look to be two perfectly ordinary toilet compartments reveal a hidden secret. The first one contains a perfectly standard toilet, just like the type you would find in an aircraft built in Toulouse or Seattle. I don't know why, but I decide to have a look in the second one too, like a cop looking for a hidden fugitive. And my instinct pays off.

There is a further door inside this one, which leads to a hidden room containing a powerful-looking shower, normally an unknown pleasure for the long-range rail adventurer. I plan to make good use of this in the morning.

After a couple of hours we reach the Polish border at Terespol, and I have no trouble from the Polish security team searching the train before it crosses over the River Bug to the Belarus side. This is where my Belarus transit visa kicks in, and gives me 48 hours to cross into the Russian Federation. Once the train is over the river, officers in different uniforms take their turn to inspect the passengers and their belongings. I must have made a few schoolboy errors on my entry paperwork, as an excitable officer marches back and forth with my form asking for more information a couple of times. But when his boss arrives, he seems more relaxed and stamps my visa, wishing me well. The customs people are pretty thorough and search deep into my big bag. The officer pulls out a small brown paper parcel and asks me what it is. I struggle to know how to explain this to him as I don't yet know myself. Before I'd set off Keith Parsons had given me this as a gift. A handwritten label is attached to it by string saying that it's a Red Cross parcel from the Edinburgh Explorer's Club. I suspect that it contains illicit booze, but had not intended to open it until I reached Manchuria. Without thinking too much about the implications of my answer, I shrug my shoulders apologetically and say I don't know what's in it. Can you imagine doing this at Heathrow Airport? The rubber gloves would be out before you could say 'drug mule'. Here, the official takes a long look at me, then a long look at the parcel, as if the choice of wrapping paper might indicate its content. Then he thrusts it back at me like he's bored, or someone has just announced that his tea's ready. It would seem I'm off the hook, and before long we are shunted out of the frontier and backwards to the sheds where we get off so that they can change the bogies for the wider gauge tracks of the Russian Federation.

Inside the huge engine shed I can see orange boiler-suited workers busily attending to the underside of our train. Each carriage is uncoupled and pushed onto a production line. First of all, they disconnect the bogies and raise each carriage into the air with a pair of hydraulic lifts, and then cables pull the narrower bogies away and new wider ones into their place on a second set of tracks. Finally, the carriage is lowered back down and reconnected to the train before being pulled back out of the shed by a new locomotive. The process takes about an hour to complete for all the carriages that make up our train. In the future this line will be served by new trains with an adjustable gauge, but today we are part of this time-honoured tradition.

High visibility vests and hard hats seem surplus to the workers' requirements. The men are instead protected from injury by their super-warm traditional ushanka hats and cheap cigarettes. As the bogie-changing process tends to amaze people unaccustomed to them, I take some suitably moody photographs out of the door at the end of the carriage. Lira doesn't seem to like me doing this and I can't work out why. I think it might be that she considers the bogie technology of our new Austrian train to be a state secret. But then I wonder if she is trying to hide the reality that modern Russia still has men in fur hats performing jobs like this. I ignore her and keep taking pictures until she decides to push in front of me, obscuring my view. It's clearly not worth fighting over, so I move out the way until she disappears back into her little control room. I would really like to get a smile out of her before the train reaches Moscow, but – now especially – I might have my work cut out.

Local time has moved on a couple of hours, so it's not until about 3.30 am that we are under way again. There has been little point trying to get to sleep before we depart, as the rough shunting of each carriage back onto the train results in huge crashes that knock everything over in my compartment.

I sleep fitfully through the rest of the night and don't rise until 10.30 the next morning. Throughout the night I vaguely recall hearing a switch being pushed and a loud beeping noise before it is switched off again. I think this has something to do with the lack of power in my compartment this morning. But this holds no fear for me as I carry a big lithium battery in my bag that can recharge all my devices several times over.

My morning ablution routine when on the rails usually involves a trip to the toilet to make the best use possible of the extremely limited facilities. A few drips of cold water above a tiny sink is quite normal, so I carry a few packs of wet wipes. But this morning I remember my discovery and head down the corridor with the glee of a small boy on bath night at boarding school. It's time for a shower. And it works marvellously. Clean and fresh for the day ahead, I repack my kit and explore the outer ends of the carriage to see what's going on. At the far end of our coach, another railway miracle has taken place overnight; despite what I have been told, a Russian restaurant carriage has been hooked up after the border. It's located right next door to carriage 344 and is a step back to the cold war, the very opposite of the swanky new sleeper carriages. Once through the hatch-like door of the creaky wooden-panelled carriage, I'm greeted by a friendly old chef who seems surprised to see me. Perhaps I should have made a reservation. The next few moments are comedy gold, as we don't have a word in common and I have misplaced my vital 'point at it' picture book, which has pictures of almost anything you can think of, and which I use to communicate. Instead I reach for the Russian translator app on my phone, but it is totally useless for ordering breakfast. Chef does a better impression of a chicken than I do of chicken eggs, but thankfully before I agree on a random breakfast of his creation, he finds a menu with some English handwritten underneath each of the options. I dine on fried eggs, chopped ham and onions served with stale dark bread and thick coffee. Chef seems happy to have something to do other than smoke his little roll-ups.

Late in the morning we make a stop at a deserted station without any obvious name. Hopping off to get some fresh air, I see that the most notice-able thing from the platform is that our train is much shorter than it was yesterday. Just four sleeper carriages and the restaurant car remain; all the seated carriages must have been sent back to Poland at the border. Lira waves at me to get back on board, and we set off again, chugging through the murky Russian countryside. I don't think she has forgiven me yet for my espionage in the engine shed, but she remains professional, if not very friendly. With nothing to do for a couple of hours I make a cup of tea and sit back with a good book. It's Roald Dahl's 'Going Solo'.

Moscow is a massive city. By population it's the fifth or sixth largest in the world, and you really get to appreciate this when arriving by train. The line skirts around the suburbs before heading inwardsto the heart of the metropolis. Dozens of railway lines converge as the network of tracks lead us towards Belorussky station, our destination. Old and new buildings reach up to the sky side by side; brutalist apartment blocks and Stalinist skyscrapers are now next door to ultra-modern tower blocks. Lira returns my ticket as we crawl the final few hundred metres to the platform. Her frown almost turns into a smile as I thank her for looking after me, but years of training in looking miserable take over instinctively, and she stops herself just in time. The city has yet to freeze up for the winter, and the platform is a sea of dirty slush; this can be quite lethal, as it refreezes each night to form a layer of black ice. Things get much easier when everything is frozen solid and cleaned up for the winter, but here the temperatures so far this winter have yet to fall far enough for this to happen. In the open-air concourse, I look out for a taxi driver – it's not hard to do as the taxi touts find you. There is no taxi rank; instead, men in leather coats approach and offer the services of drivers who loiter out front by the unregulated car park. I know the drill here, and it only takes me a couple of minutes to find someone to take me to where I'm staying at a price that sounds reasonable. But the big unknown is how they have been taught to drive. Muscovite taxi drivers come from two main schools, the getaway drivers and the grand prix drivers. The chance of survival is roughly equal with both, but the getaway drivers will scare you with late turns and bac street manoeuvres, rather than pure straight line speed. A couple of minutes into the trip and our family saloon is ploughing through the early evening traffic, my driver freely using both his horn and his hand brake. He's from the getaway school, I suspect, majoring in stunt driving. In the back seat I tighten my seatbelt, lean back and smile. I'm back in the USSR.

Chapter Seven:
Vostok

On 11 April 1961 Vostok 1 took off from Baikonur Cosmodrome in what is now Kazakhstan, carrying Yuri Gagarin into a low Earth orbit, making him the first human being to travel into space. You can still see the capsule that returned Gagarin safely to Earth in the Energia museum in the outskirts of Moscow. Vostok means 'east', and the train that will take me to Manchuria and beyond has been bestowed with the same name. I have two whole days to prepare for my next journey. When you have been on the rails for even just a couple of days, the simple pleasures of staying in a modern hotel are that much more rewarding.

Although I very much like being in Moscow, part of the pleasure I get from being here is actually derived from the alienation that I feel as someone who speaks little Russian. You have to depend on the kindness of strangers, and every successful transaction can be celebrated as a success of non-verbal communication. A trip on the city's metro system is a good challenge to test these skills. Once you have managed to buy a ticket using just fingers, and then survived the vicious turnstiles, you have to learn a whole new ball game of navigation. Only some of the maps have English translations, and each station can have several different names, one for each line that it serves. When I was first in Moscow, I'd used the colours of the lines and counted stops, but as my confidence grew I began to learn the sounds of the station names and how they appeared in Cyrillic. You can identify some stations by the shape of the number of lines crossing, turning the map into a big geometric puzzle. But lose concentration for a split second and you can become hopelessly lost. Never mind. The architecture of every stop is both unique and amazing to those of us more familiar with the Northern Line. I must once have spent most of a day admiring stations without even surfacing.

Tucked away from the main tourist attractions of the city is a rather bizarre part of the Soviet Union's space programme. In November 1988 the CCCP launched a reusable spacecraft weighing over 100 tonnes into orbit. It took off without any cosmonauts on board, and was successfully landed by remote control three hours later. If you showed anyone from the west a picture of it, they would tell you it was the NASA space shuttle, but to those behind the iron curtain it was pure Soviet engineering, and known as the Buran. (As with the TU-144 and Concorde, and the Yakovlev Yak-38 and the Harrier jump jet, the Russian versions and the western ones were very similar-looking.) Only one Buran ever flew in space, but there were several test versions used to simulate missions and train its crew. Of the two that survive today, one is now kept in a backlot of VDNKh, an exhibition park in the heart of Moscow.

Armed with a steaming cup of mulled wine, I search for the Buran in a place I have been directed to by a lady selling candyfloss. The darkness is actually quite spacelike, and when I spot it all I can see are spotlights illuminating the nose and wings. Wandering around at first, and then underneath its belly, I find some stairs up to the flight deck. They are the kind of stairs that small airports use to disembark cheap charter flights, and they just about meet up with a hatch in the side of the Buran towards the flight deck. The hatch is closed today, but I wonder if it's locked. Why would you need a lock on the outside of a spacecraft door? I'm the only person here showing any interest in the Buran, and a man wanders over to find out what I'm up to. He tells me that you can normally pay to go in, but only after they have weighed you. He thinks that I'm going to be too heavy, but isn't precise about the dieting goal that would be needed to get on board. With my cosmonaut dreams in tatters, I head back to my hotel to contemplate the midnight express to Manchuria.

The Vostok leaves Moscow's Yaraslovsky station every Saturday night at close to midnight. Unlike the modern Leningradsky station building next door, Yaraslovsky isn't a particularly sophisticated place, and when I arrive I find a few drunks outside, ready to greet me. I dodge them as best as I can and slip into the entrance of the station building. The officers doing the security check inside the doors are dressed for action, wearing shiny bomber jackets and ushanka hats. I wonder what they're looking for. My bags slowly pass through the x-ray scanner. The man by the machine should be able to see my cornucopia of knives, needles, pills and booze, but he doesn't pass comment or raise the alarm. Instead I'm directed to pick my bags off the belt and carry on about my business. In the open-plan concourse there are a couple of shops selling pastries and magazines, a ticket office and a seating area under a departure board. All the seats I can see are taken, loaded up with soldiers and piles of their kit.

Well stocked up from my local Sokolniki supermarket, I now have an extra couple of bags containing assorted noodles, biscuits and porridge, as well as a stash of reasonable Spanish wine. I can just about carry it all, with a wobbling motion and the right balance. A kind lady overseeing the 'special needs' seating area waves me over and invites me sit down in her roped-off zone. Here I join families, the old and the infirm. The people around me are very friendly, and passengers take it in turn to look after each other's belongings whilst they conduct last-minute shopping. In a eureka moment I manage to decrypt most the Cyrillic words on the departure board. The trick is to stop trying too hard to read it, and then as if by magic the words somehow start to appear: Moscow, Harbin, Peking, Vostok. I need to be on platform 1.

No one else seems to be heading out into the cold yet, but I can't stand the thought of missing the train, so it's a form of mental torture to wait in the warmth of the station any longer. Trudging through the snow around to the far side of the station, I can hear a woman speaking on the public address system. Her tunes and announcements bounce off the snow, and echo around the platforms. Of course I have no idea what she's saying, but I like the jingle noise at the start of each of her announcements. Here in Russia it's the same sound, no matter if you're in Moscow or Murmansk, Vladimir or Vladivostok. It makes me inwardly smile to wonder if she might have a xylophone or similar percussion instrument on standby as a backup.

Approaching the platform, I'm greeted by the distinctive smell of burning coal. It triggers my excitement about adventure on the rails. Not the romanticism of steam engines, but coal being burned to heat up the carriage samovars. Even a modern-day Trans-Siberian train needs coal. I assume that this is to ensure there is always a heat source if there is no electricity from an attached powered locomotive. Adequate heating isn't a luxury but a requirement for survival in the heart of Siberia.

Platform 1 is tucked around a corner from all the other regular platforms, perhaps because its trains are more irregular. Only a small proportion of Russian trains are international, and this is certainly one of them. In front of me is the rear end of train number 020, the Vostok. There is always a moment of apprehension when you meet a new train for the first time, especially one that you will be spending a long time living on. Not all carriages are created equal in the game of roulette that is the carriage numbering system, when the difference of one digit can mean a compartment in a carriage 30 years older than the one next door. Then there is the randomness of the staff in one carriage being amazing and in the one next door power-crazy sociopaths. I don't know it at this first moment of meeting my train, but it turns out that I can in fact relax, as this is going to be one of the best Russian trains I have ever travelled on.

Walking down the platform I'm impressed by the appearance of the train. You get to spot little things: the freshness of the paintwork, the cleanliness of the windows, glimpses of the décor inside. Whilst not brand new like my train from Poland, the carriages are all modern and well taken care of. Smartly dressed staff are on parade to greet passengers on the platform outside each carriage. At carriage number 4 I meet a lady called Rima. She immediately breaks apart my Russian Railways provodnitsa stereotype. Taking my ticket, she smiles at me, marks me as present on her manifest and welcomes me on board. She introduces me to a man called Sergei, who stands behind inside the entrance to the carriage. He is a well-presented man in his thirties wearing a carefully pressed RZD uniform and coloured designer glasses. He looks like he might work for a start-up airline rather than a state railway. I'm also pretty surprised to discover that he speaks some English. This has never happened to me on a Russian train before, and it's an unexpected bit of good news. In one fell swoop I'm deprived of the fun of sign language, but instead will benefit from knowing much more about what's going on as we head east.

Left to my own devices, I unpack and try out all the switches and knobs in my two-berth SV (first-class) compartment. Everything seems to work, apart from the small plasma screen, but I won't be needing that; I'm not a fan of the sort of films that get shown on Russian television. But best of all, above the big window there is a small one that opens inwards, and it is unlocked. The only thing that is missing here is a power socket, but there are several in the corridor.

Satisfied that everything is in order I pull my gear on and get back onto the platform to take the obligatory photograph of the train before we set off. Rima, now on the platform too, understands and doesn't seem too concerned. She must be used to seeing travellers hopping off for a cigarette. Wandering down the outside of the train I locate the restaurant carriage, just one in front, and then a series of kupe (four-berth) sleepers. Looking through my camera's viewfinder I try to get a suitably artistic shot of the carriages in the snow and artificial light. In the background I can hear the distant revving of an engine followed by the mechanical sound that carriages make when taking up the tension of being pulled. The train is on the move without me. I only have a couple of seconds' panic, though, as looking down the platform I see a shunter adding more carriages before the proper Vostok locomotive arrives. Soon running out of freshly artistic angles for my photographs, I put the camera back in my bag. I hang out with Rima until I can no longer feel my fingertips.

It's always nice to get back inside a toasty warm carriage when the temperature outside is well below zero. Climbing back on board, I turn right and through the inner doors into the carpeted corridor. At station stops it is standard operating procedure to cover the carpet with a single long cloth to prevent new passengers from treading snow and ice into it. Once you are settled in you wear indoor footwear – Russians mostly wear flip-flops. The door to the platform only gets opened at one end of the carriage, and it is at this end, too, that the samovar is bubbling away ready to provide hot water for endless cups of tea and bowls of noodles. At the other end are the two toilets and a door through to the next carriage. My compartment is in the middle, which will be perfect for a smooth ride.

We're off, and I have a good feeling about the Vostok. Contemplating my good fortune, just when I couldn't have imagined anything could be any better, a lady from the restaurant carriage pops her head into my compartment and introduces herself. She has a basket of goodies on permanent offer: instant noodles, candy, toys, and RZD merchandise. I'm feeling like I deserve a beer, and she happily heads off to find me one. When she returns with an icy Baltika No 7, I notice that she has it hidden under her menu. I think that technically you are not allowed alcohol outside the restaurant carriage on a Russian train. However, the rule seems to be flexible if you look like you are going to behave. Or maybe it's a privilege of being in SV. I could get very used to this. My compartment has just two berths, both lower ones, and it looks like I am going to be on my own. RZD has several types of service in first class, just to confuse the frequent flyer, the very best being called business class. To be described as business class the train has to meet a variety of standards on speed, comfort and amenities on offer to passengers. Sometimes meals are included as well, but not on this train. This looks to me like almost business class, but without my own power socket and complimentary slippers.

All I have to do now is make my bed with the crisply pressed sheets and blankets provided. I decide to sleep in the forward berth, leaving the other one as a seat for use during the daytime so

I can look out towards the front. I like to maintain standards when I'm on the rails, and even though I'm not expecting a bed inspection in the morning I achieve some reasonably well-defined hospital corners. Between the beds there is a small table covered in a white linen cloth; here I lay out my alarm clock (set to Moscow time, or 'train time'), eye shade, ear plugs, torch and lucky Swiss Army penknife. With the lights turned off, all I can see now are the glowing controls above the door. They look like distant planets in an imaginary sky. Sleep doesn't come easily as I adjust to the rhythm of the rails. Outside, the bright flashes that are visible from the edges of the window blind indicate passing goods yards and stations. We pull out of our first major stop, Vladimir, at 02.52, and only then do I finally drift off. There is absolutely no pressure to be up for breakfast, or even lunch, yet I somehow feel a sense of responsibility to be up in order to supervise the routine at our major stops. This means being up in good time for Kirov later in the morning. I find that on a train journey of this length a shorter night's sleep and a short afternoon nap can work quite well. I don't know why this is; maybe just the decadence of knowing that you can sleep when you want to and set your own agenda each day.

Lifting my eyeshade in the morning, I'm greeted by bright daylight outside, shining through the window blind. The dazzling whiteness of the snow has tricked me into getting up earlier than I had planned. But this is all relative now, as the train is running on Moscow time, and already the local time is an hour or two further ahead, something that will grow every day as we make progress eastwards. I can feel the train is slowing down, almost imperceptibly at first, but a gradual deceleration that I know means we have just 5 or 10 minutes to run before arriving at the next destination on the timetable. This is a signal to me to get my boots on and find my outside clothes. I emerge from my compartment rather blearily into the bright sunshine on the other side of the train. Sergei has been up and about for some time, and I can see that he's ready for the stop. Not just in a jacket, hat and gloves sort of way, but also sporting a big iron bar to attack the ice that will have built up under the carriage overnight. Once we have stopped he gets the door opened and lowers the steps to the platform. Only when he has de-iced, brushed snow off the steps and wiped the handrails am I allowed to get off. It's standard operating procedure.

Despite our being only one day east of Moscow, the temperature has dropped noticeably overnight. The digital thermometer under the station clock on platform 1 reads -13°C. Worse still, the fresh snow covers black ice, and I take about ten steps along the platform towards the locomotive before falling onto my knees and making a fool of myself in front of a group of tough-looking soldiers. But they smoke their cigarettes contentedly and smile at me in a way that is friendly and unthreatening. They would look even tougher if they put their boots on. It's obviously not very cold for them, as they are clad in a strange dress code of combats and plastic slippers.

There is a definite sense of comradeship between passengers on a Russian train. It doesn't matter how you dress or what language you speak; train travellers, like those at sea, behave like a community on the move. Anyone on the train is welcome to smoke or just hang out as part of the group whenever we stop. So now, without confidence in my ability to stay upright, I give up my plan to visit the engine, and stay with the soldiers. We stamp our feet and keep our limbs moving to keep the blood flowing to any chilled bits of flesh. After 20 minutes an unloaded mail truck grinds back down the platform towards us, signalling that it's time to get back aboard. I say goodbye to my new friends and carefully slide towards the next carriage, where Sergei stands waiting for the signal from the train master to close up. I don't know what his official title is, but 'train master' feels appropriate. Not wishing to get in anyone's bad books for delaying our departure, I climb back aboard the Vostok.

There is a definite routine to life on a long-distance train, and none more so than those that cross Siberia. The day is defined by two main activities: getting off the train whenever it stops, and visiting the restaurant carriage. In between these events come other occasional activities: consulting the map, writing, reading, and chatting to anyone who shares a common language. I'm not blessed in the language department, and other than English I can only manage a bit of schoolboy French and Thai, which isn't very helpful for this journey. The days are short, made even shorter each time we pass into a new time zone. My routine tends to be breakfast late and not to eat lunch. Instead, after breakfast I use the samovar in our carriage to make reasonable coffee or strange-tasting Russian instant soup for the rest of the day. Then in the evening I explore the range of dishes on the menu in the restaurant, washed down with a couple of beers.

Mid-morning seems to be the most social time of the day on the train. This is when you meet people at the samovar making tea or in the corridor returning from their ablutions. For me, a chance to meet the other occupants of carriage number 4 for the first time. At the far end to me live a friendly Russian middle-aged couple. He smokes a lot and she likes trashy soap operas, which she plays loudly on her laptop. In between us is a soldier, who has a compartment to himself. He's a young officer, and in my imagination, the Kremlin are sending him on a special mission somewhere very hush hush. Perhaps his orders are still sealed in his shiny and rather un-tactical leather briefcase. At the other end of the carriage, next to where Sergei and Rima live, are a couple of Kiwi travellers, Neil and Pat. Wherever you are off the beaten track in this world you tend to find Kiwis. They have a wonderful spirit of adventure and are quite fearless of places that most would never consider visiting – it must be all that fresh air and fine Pinot Noir. The other compartments remain empty for the time being.

It's far too early to guess what Sergei makes of me, but I think he realises that I might have played this game before. As with some sort of higher-order Masonic secret, I indicate quietly to him that I know about the secret cupboard in the outer compartment at the end of our carriage. Its official purpose is probably to keep emergency equipment like flags and a lantern – but, at a steady temperature just above freezing, it is also the perfect place to chill white wine and store cheese. We don't do a funny handshake, but he knows exactly what I want to do, and produces a special key to open it up. I actually already have my own copy of this key, but I don't feel it is very respectful to the chain of command to admit this, at least not at this point in our relationship. It's the same key that opens the window in my compartment and allows me to reduce the temperature in my compartment to about 20°C – or well below freezing if I get it wrong and the window freezes in the open position. Window opening is an activity that I only perform under the cover of darkness, always reclosing it before any major stops. Ice quickly forms where moisture from my breath hits the freezing outside world, and this needs to be carefully removed before the window can be properly resealed. I have a special tool for this purpose. It's an unmodified RZD first-class coat hanger.

As the day passes we get ever closer to the Ural Mountains and the geographical beginnings of Siberia. Although it's completely unnecessary, I like to get my map out several times each day and chart our progress. It feels good, if perhaps a little Victorian. I have marked the interesting places on our route and can plot our steady progress eastwards. We travel at a slow but constant speed, but by being on the move for perhaps 22 hours of every day, the train is covering around 1000 kilometres every 24 hours. It's dark by 15.30 Moscow time, and shortly after 16.00 we arrive at Balezino. It's a really small town, but one with a vital purpose for Trans-Siberian passengers, as here the electrified line switches from

AC to DC, so we need a new locomotive before we can travel any further east. Whilst this is being organised we take on coal, water and the mail. I have time to shuffle up to the front of the train and watch all that is going on, hoping not to be taken for a trainspotter. I don't think that trainspotting is a well understood hobby here – maybe train numbers were once classified as a state secret in the CCCP– so my cover is as a traveller taking exercise on the platform. Careful not to fall over again, I make it as far as the locomotive, perhaps ten carriages in front of mine. The snow here in Balezino is now firmer and more compacted, so not slippery, and from here through Siberia will stay like this for the rest of the winter.

The driver of the departing AC locomotive looks down at me from his monstrous red machine. I'm the only human being down below, dwarfed by the scale of the train towering above me. Trying to work out what I'm up to, he opens his door and shouts down at me in what sounds like friendly Russian. I tell him my name and where I am from, and then we do some waving. I wonder for a moment if he's inviting me on board his beast, but this has all sorts of complications, as he has uncoupled and is about to take his train back to the engine sheds of Kirov for the night. Meanwhile my belongings are on the Vostok, next stop Perm, so playing it safe, I opt to stay alongside it on the platform, where I am kept company by a small gang of stray dogs until the new locomotive arrives. The dogs follow me around in case I might have food, or indeed if I might become be a food source should the cold eventually incapacitate me. Communication isn't possible as they don't understand English. They ignore my commands and sniff my feet, as though they might be my most tasty body part.

When Sergei sees the dogs he shoos them away with some Russian that they obviously do understand. He beckons me back up the steps as, with no more passengers to get on, he wants to shut up the carriage. A minute or two later we creak and jolt as the Vostok breaks its inertia and slowly moves off. Back inside the carriage, overheating is an immediate possibility, so I peel off some layers as soon as I reach the inner corridor. Sliding my compartment door open I'm greeted by the sight of a covering of fine powdered snow that has covered every surface. Perhaps the tiny opening that I created in my window wasn't such a good idea. I'm not sure if Sergei would be angry or just laugh at the thin blanket of snow on my bed, so I close the door before anyone spots my winter wonderland. The clean-up operation is mostly effective, although my bed remains a bit damp. But as if this wasn't bad enough, the kinetic tensioning of the carriages as we accelerate creates a series of shock waves as they catch up with the engine and snatch back again. The contents of my compartment are shaken about and I manage to cover myself from head to toe in a glass of quite reasonable merlot. I spend the rest of the evening mopping up wine, snow and red snow from most surfaces of the compartment before turning in for the night.

The next morning when I emerge from my cocoon, Rima is busy vacuuming outside. I feel vaguely guilty about having a lie-in, until I subtract three hours from my clock and work out that in local time it's actually respectably early. I fall into the routine of sorting myself and get my gear out ready for our first stop of the day, at Ishim. Sergei is already in the outer compartment at the end of the carriage as we approach the station. I'm learning that he can be a man of few words, but his English is clear. He breaks it down into two words for me today, 'Cold, problem.' I'm not sure of the nature of the problem and if it means just a minor issue or imminent global thermonuclear war. But fortunately, it turns out to be that the outer door of the train has frozen shut overnight. Whilst this would be a problem for you or me to fix, Sergei has a range of heavy metal implements to beat it into submission. He chooses a suitably heavy wrench and starts hitting it until he finds the sweet spot which encourages it to open. Rima looks on, assessing his technique and choice of tools. They must cover this problem in RZD training school.

My time at Ishim, where the stop is only scheduled to last for 10 minutes, is focused on getting a resupply of drinking water. This is because although I use water from the samovar to make hot drinks, when cooled it has a brackish colour, and tastes oily to me – and the option of drinking water directly from one of the cold-water taps on board would definitely be a very bad idea. Siberian platform shops are a strange retail phenomenon, and a concept that I think it is safe to say will never catch on with major western retailers. The kiosks have a glass window plastered full of every item on sale and, low down, a tiny hatch used to peer in and conduct business though. A bit of pointing and proffering some roubles results in a transaction, and the item is passed out to you though the hatch. The excitement of retail therapy overtakes my common sense, and I also buy some chocolate, a rather kitsch decorative plate and a freshly cooked doughnut that turns out to be stuffed with meat and vegetables. This actually tastes pretty good, and I conclude that if it's still warm in this climate, it must have been freshly made. The first stop of the morning is the most important one to me. Fresh air in the lungs, bright light and meeting other passengers lifts my spirits and puts me in a good mood for the day ahead. But this morning there isn't much time to hang around and exchange pleasantries as we're not taking on coal or mail here. The driver blows his horn, Sergei waves at me, and I hop back on the icy steps that lead up into our carriage in the nick of time. The train is rolling before the door is closed.

Two carriages forward from my home is the social centre of the train, the restaurant carriage. Like many in use on the Trans-Siberian, it's older and a little shabbier than the modern sleeper carriages either side of it. My understanding is that these are run as a separate business from the rest of the train, and although they have a similar menu across the network, everything is down to the people who run it. Many things on the rather extensive menu tend not to be available, but you never know what is possible if you don't ask.

Without thinking, I break my train rule number 5 – never wash your hands just before passing between carriages in Siberia – and quickly regret it. Wet hands stick super-rapidly to the frozen metal handles on the outside ends of each coach. Some of the carriage crossings are quite challenging, requiring a hop across the snow-covered twisting metal ramp in the no man's land between coaches. This takes some practice; it's all about timing and anticipating the movement of the train. Arriving at the outer door of restaurant carriage, it's very obvious that it is rolling stock alien to the rest of the train. The sleeper carriages have hydraulic opening door systems with the press of a button, but here the big grey enamelled door that looks like it's from a submarine is opened by a tug on the handles. Ouch! Inside, the first noticeable difference is the smell of cooking fat, but the layout is very different too, with a corridor along one side past the kitchen, then an open space containing four-seat booths along both sides. At the far end is a bar where people can buy snacks, and possibly also illicit black-market goods. The restaurant manager is called Valerie. Today he is seated at the booth nearest the bar, busy counting money and adding things up with an enormous desk calculator. It takes him a while to notice me, but eventually he approaches to enquire if I want a beer. Even on local time it's not noon yet, so I decline his offer, and study the menu complete with rather weird English translations.

Valerie turns out to be one of the nicest and most sincere people that I have ever met on a Russian train. Like Sergei and Rima, he smiles more than most Russian railway employees do, but he also takes enormous pride in everything he does. He's not a snappy dresser, but someone has told him to always wear a tie and a name badge. He speaks only a little English, but has a warm soul that wants to help you; he might bring you sugar to go with your escalope or tomato sauce for your tea, but he always means well. At my table today, we dance our usual dance. What would I like to eat? I point at a variety of things but they are met with an apologetic shrug. Not today. 'Caviar?' I ask. Surely not, but his face lights up and he beams a gold-toothed smile. Scribbling something on his little pad he heads back to the kitchen and leaves me to stare out the window, an occupation that can absorb hours before you realise what you are doing. My caviar arrives shortly, together with herb butter, blinis and a cup of Russian-style coffee. It's like Turkish coffee, where the grounds get mixed in with the water and sugar and sink to the bottom, forming a thick sludge on the bottom of your cup. Two cups of this rocket fuel together with the caviar and blinis cost me just 500 roubles, about £4.50. It's the bargain of the trip so far.

As passengers pass through the carriage, most of them enjoy a loud and enthusiastic conversation with Valerie. He appears to be a lifelong friend to some of them. Even the on-board policemen stop for a chat with him. They seem to ask him a lot of questions, and make notes in their little black books. Have they heard about the hidden black-market vodka? I know where it is, as I'm sitting on top of it. Each of the bench seats has a smuggler's compartment underneath. Hoping I'm not going to be arrested by association with the booze, I ignore the cops and swirl my thick coffee around in my chipped cup as though I'm going to tell my fortune with the grounds stuck to the bottom.

At this moment the boiler-suited engineer enters the carriage and walks towards the bar. I don't know what his official job description is, but he seems to be the first response to any flooding or heating problems when we're on the move. Today he has assembled a long hose onto what looks like an enema bag. He sees me staring at his apparatus and mutters 'systemia, systemia' to me apologetically as he walks past. I fear it's to do with the pressurised toilets on board, but I'm probably better off not knowing.

I have been on Trans-Siberian trains in the past that are packed with foreign travellers. The atmosphere on board can be party-like. It's huge fun, but somehow this can also make the experience feel a little less authentic; the splendid isolation and loneliness of the

long-distance rail traveller is somehow lost.
We all seek that unique journey, that feeling that
we are pioneers of the route. But now, here
on the Vostok, I'm pretty much on my own with
just the Kiwis for English-speaking company.
When we stop at Omsk in the early afternoon
the peace and solitude is broken by prospective
cabin mates attempting to load their belongings
onto the train. I use the word 'prospective' as
I'm amazed how many people try to get into
our carriage without a valid ticket, or for that
matter any ticket. They either can't read their
ticket, or they are after a free ride. Rima isn't
having any of this, and she sends them packing
before they can push their bags up through
the outer door.

Our platform at Omsk is a busy place. The city was
once the home to the Russian Empire's gold reserves
and then became the main Soviet production
centre of the T-80 tank. Today it is the biggest
city in western Siberia, and its oil wealth has
been carved up by the former party élite to form
privatised industrial conglomerates. Crowds
of people congregate around our train. The
sailors stand out in their blue disruptive camouflage
uniforms, but not as much as the ice hockey
team on tour. Wandering amongst them I have
some unanswered questions for Sergei. Why
are there so many sailors on a landlocked train?

Is an ice hockey stick excess baggage on a train? The stop here is for just 16 minutes, but after 5 of them my beard is quite frosty and I'm keen to get back on board. Rima smiles at me from deep inside the hood of her RZD issue coat, and helps me back up the steel-and-ice climbing frame that allows access to the carriage from the ground when there are no proper platforms.

Settling back in my compartment, I read about the history of Manchuria and drink tea. My guide book describes Outer Manchuria, the wider region outside China, as a 'cockpit of conflict', and at first it feels like one of those bad history lessons at school when nothing seems to make sense. To make progress in my studies I have to look up the Russo-Japanese War, the Chinese Civil War and the Korean War. I will be interested to see if the ground today looks like it was worth all that fighting for. My reading is interrupted by Rima, who always passes with her vacuum cleaner in the afternoon just before it gets dark. Taking pride in the cleanliness of our carriage, she hoovers out each compartment as well as the corridor, so I vacate to allow her to complete her duties. There are probably not many scheduled trains in the world where your compartment gets cleaned like this each day.

The evening passes in time-honoured fashion with a trip to see Valerie in the restaurant. He's there when I arrive, hovering around tables with his mighty Casio calculator and notepad. The sailors and the ice hockey players are nowhere to be seen, but some locals are sitting at the tables eating pickled gherkins and drinking little carafes of vodka. I try a bit of sign language and hold some flimsy conversations with the aid of my 'point at it' picture book. I also take the opportunity to try out my phone app, which says key phrases out loud. The problem with this is that the voice is a bit creepy, and all the phrases seem to have been created for the Russian dating scene. Deciding that this is too high-risk in present company, I put it away and go back to some more miming. Drinking with the locals can become an endless pastime, one that gets trickier to escape from the further in you get. Sensing potential carnage, I elect to say goodnight before it goes too far, and head back to my compartment for an early night. Fully acclimatised to the steady movement of the train, I quickly fall into deep and comfortable sleep of strange rail-related dreams.

There is an unmistakable aroma of bacon and eggs in my compartment when I wake the following morning. Unless I now have the sense of smell of cooked breakfasts in my dreams, I think that Sergei must be making his own breakfast in the fire of our carriage samovar. I have read that some people dream in black and white, but I dream in colour and also in stereo. But

I can't remember ever smelling anything in a dream. Getting up takes a bit of determination, but as we are due to stop soon in Krasnoyarsk I need to get going. My plan here this morning is a simple one. There is a 22-minute window for resupply of my on-board larder and maybe also time for some light exercise. Multitasking, I manage to brush my teeth whilst getting dressed before we pull into the station. For such a large place there isn't much for sale on the platform, but I manage to find a little cabin selling most of what I need. It seems to specialise in trinkets and bizarre gifts, stocking an impressive range of brightly coloured flip-flops and stuffed oversized cuddly animals. With the sun up and clear blue sky it's bracing outside, and the warmth of direct sunshine on the exposed parts of my body is unexpectedly good.

Krasnoyarsk grew as a city with the arrival of the Trans-Siberian railway in the 1890s, but is perhaps better known historically for its Cossacks and its gulags. The main feature of the city is that it's bisected by the mighty Yenisei river, and as we leave the station behind I'm treated to a spectacular view of its waters as we traverse the open girders of the bridge. The river is actually warmer than the land, and an eerie layer of mist rises up from the water. As if I'm competing in a rail-based game of I-Spy, I point this out to Valerie. As always, he's in a good mood and is happy to talk to me whilst I enjoy my ham and eggs. He explains that he lives nearby, and that there is a massive hydro-electric plant just up the river, meaning that it never freezes. Neither of us know the English–Russian translation for 'hydro-electric', but with ingenuity he gets his wallet out and shows me an illustration of it on the back of a 10-rouble banknote. Consulting my various timekeeping devices, I realise that I have in fact eaten my breakfast at lunchtime locally. I resolve to try harder with the time zone changes; had I lingered at table much longer it would have been dinnertime in Beijing.

Chapter Eight:
Into the Heart of Manchuria

Arriving back at carriage number 4, I realise that I have a slightly tricky situation to manage. It appears that my secret window-opening activities have been rumbled. The window in my compartment has been sealed and locked in my absence. I'm guessing this has been done by Sergei, but he's not saying anything about it and I have to pretend of course that I haven't done anything. My dilemma is that I have the key to open it up again, but before today I could have just pretended it had always been unlocked. Now if I'm found out, they will know that I must have the key. I'm annoyed with myself for not being more discreet. The temperature in my compartment has become a stuffy 28°C, just the way Russian passengers love it. I decide to strip off and leave things as they are until the cover of darkness.

It has been getting progressively colder outside. I can almost feel the warm humid air being sucked out of my lungs as I cough and splutter when making the perilous jump between carriages. Using Sergei's carriage thermometer, the readings are now around -25°C during the day. The climate is brutal in these parts. The record low in Siberia is -52.8°C, but in the summer months it can be as hot as 36°C. Our current conditions are perhaps best summed up by Neil, the Kiwi chap who lives down the corridor. Back at Ishim I'd overheard him report back to his wife after our afternoon stop there: 'My feet are all right, my legs are a bit numb, but it's my face that I can't feel.' I'm wondering if the beer in the fridge of the restaurant carriage will be warmer than the supplies in the unheated cupboard next door. My beer of choice this trip is Baltika No 7. It proudly pronounces on the tin, 'Made by Russians'. I think advertising standards would prevent this line being used by most international brands today, unless they could prove the single pure nationality of their workforce.

Rolling into Novosibirsk for the final stop of the day there doesn't seem to be much going on in the darkness outside. But this is the third biggest city in Russia, the Chicago of Siberia on the banks of the River Ob, and with its own great lake. On the platform there are just a few hardy souls indulging in a quick smoke, so where is everyone hiding? The answer is that most passengers lurk in waiting rooms to protect themselves from the climate until their trains arrive.

I will remember the capital city of Siberia not for its nocturnal sights but for its sounds; through the thin metal skin of the carriage the soundtrack is the crunch of boots in the deeply frozen snow, the muffled wails of the station announcer, the thud of the engineers beating the bogies with their metal poles, and eventually, the short sharp toot of the horn as the driver signals our departure. Safely locked inside my compartment, I fish into my bag for the secret key and open a tiny gap in the window. Blissfully cold fresh air blasts in from the outside world.

I read somewhere that Apollo astronauts found it very difficult to sleep inside the lunar excursion module on the surface of the moon because the unfamiliar noises of mechanical systems made most of them, unsurprisingly, too jumpy. The Vostok makes odd noises too, but after a few days getting used to them, I'm able to screen them out. I now find the rhythms and mechanical sounds strangely soporific.

My breakfast is delayed the next morning as I have lost the restaurant carriage. Overnight the configuration of the train has changed as some carriages have been removed and new ones added. When I find Rima, sweeping out the coal from the samovar, she points me in the opposite direction. The dining car is now positioned behind all the kupe sleeper carriages at the very end of the train so that it can be more easily detached at the Chinese border. Sitting in my usual seat, the one that all the vodka is stashed underneath, I order coffee and get my book out. It's by Ran Fiennes, and titled 'Cold'. It seemed appropriate material for the journey, but if you don't know what he did to his frostbitten fingers with an angle grinder, it turns out not to be one for the breakfast table. Turning the page, I get that strange sensation that something is not quite the same as when I went to bed, but I can't put my finger on it. A fleeting glance out the window forces me to put the book down immediately and gawp in absolute amazement. The forests have vanished. If there has been one landscape certainty of the journey so far it has been the endless trees and snow. But now just yards from the railway line is a vast frozen sea. I have seen Lake Baikal before, but never like this. The Vostok runs on different timings to many of the other Trans-Siberian trains, and this time I'm up earlier, well before we reach Irkutsk. This rewards me with incredible views as the train skirts the foreshore of the lake. The water is frozen, and so are the little lapping waves at the edge that must have frozen in an instant as the water touched the bank. The thing that is most amazing about it, though, is the scale of it. Ice stretches out to a perfectly flat horizon with no visible sign of the other side of the lake.

I'm transfixed by the view at first, but Valerie brings my coffee over and insists on chatting whilst Chef organises my blinis. This restaurant has become my favourite place on the train; I feel very welcome here and have learned to love the almost comedic quality of much of what goes on – something between a Russian version of 'Fawlty Towers' and 'Robin's Nest'. But today, other than myself the only other customer here is a thickset Russian man sitting opposite me, slurping a bowl of solyanka accompanied by a small carafe of vodka. Then a range of officials pass through, and I wonder about their occupations on the train. Last night a chap in full military dress uniform, complete with a leather attaché case, showed up in the restaurant and produced some paperwork for completion. Sometimes I see our train police force on patrol: three officers, two men and a woman, dressed in shiny black bomber jackets and ushanka hats. Then there are the RZD employees, the provodnitsas, the engineers, and the 'fix it' men.

Before leaving I make the rash decision to break another of my previously hard rules on long-range rail adventure. Rule number 7, never look inside the kitchen of a train restaurant. Past experiences have taught me that it's generally just best not to know the scale of the bacterial load that is being served with your food. I have even begun to subscribe to the idea that a small dose of bacteria might be good at building immunity to local bugs. It's a coping strategy. But stepping inside this kitchen door I'm greeted by something quite unexpected. The room is as big as the restaurant itself and has several huge stainless steel commercial fridges along the back wall. They are so clean that they sparkle in the bright overhead light. On the worktop there are sets of gleaming knives and colour-coded chopping boards, neatly stacked and labelled. This must be the cleanest kitchen in Siberia.

But I'm not actually here to conduct a food hygiene inspection, I'm here to view the wine cellar. Many Russian restaurant carriages carry a small selection of quite interesting wines if you know what to ask for. But as I don't, a visual inspection is required; there is always the hope of discovering a rare parcel of fine wine that has been saved in case they need to cater for a high-ranking party official. Not many Russian train passengers drink wine, and I have found wines from places like the Lebanon, Georgia and Azerbaijan tucked away on past Siberian adventures. You need to get in amongst it yourself, as the wine you probably most desire often isn't the bottle that they think you might be looking for.

Valerie proudly shows me to the cupboard for storing wine and spirits. He unlocks it and shows me a few dusty bottles of sparkling wine, but there isn't much else inside. No grand crus from Tblisi or fine shiraz from Baku. There is just one rather small bottle of Russian-labelled champanski from an undisclosed region and vintage. I buy it, and I shall lay it down in my compartment for a special occasion. Valerie is apologetic about his stock levels and leads me back to the bar, where he produces some vodka from under the counter. It's a brand extension that I would never have imagined, a bottle of Kalashnikov, manufacturer of the world's most widely produced assault rifle. I try to imagine the meeting where they decided to produce vodka as a sideline to automatic weapons. This is serious diversification; the only other example that crosses my mind is English Electric, who in 1950s Great Britain started to build nuclear-capable jet fighters as well as domestic kitchen fridges. Valerie puts the vodka in a brown paper bag for me and with his gold-toothed smile wishes me a good day.

The map reveals that we won't be covering the usual distance today. I don't have any dividers with me, but an improvised piece of string reveals that it will be about a third of the average daily run. Lake Baikal is a huge obstacle in our path, and we have to skirt the shoreline southwards before continuing eastwards. Not only that, but the track is just single in places, and the westbound line is busy with freight trains carrying oil, logs and coal to the cities we have passed through. The ground shakes with the huge mass of their load, and they are so long it can take several minutes for each of them to pass by.

Irkutsk is a big stop on the Trans-Siberian. Most travellers stop here for a few days to see more of Lake Baikal, so I'm not surprised when Sergei tells me that from now on I'm the only passenger in the entire carriage. He seems a lot more chilled out today and only having one passenger to look after, he relaxes in his compartment by playing some slightly odd music. It's something like Russian techno new age disco, but I might not be doing the genre justice. In my own compartment I drink tea and update my diary whilst listening to some yacht rock. But before long I can't stop myself dozing off. The growing gap between time zones will reach its peak tomorrow, when having travelled more than one third of the way around the planet, the train will turn south for the Chinese border. But Rima wakes me in the middle of the afternoon – no one could sleep through a visit with her vacuum cleaner.

The final stop of the day is in Ulan Ude, just before sunset. The soldiers who have been in plaskart carriages further down the train unload their extensive camping gear onto the platform.They look a little less cheery today, possibly something to do with having to get off a warm train to sleep in the snow. Rather them than me. Opposite us on the same platform is another of the big Trans-Siberian trains. I think it's headed for Vladivostok. Just outside Ulan Ude is a major junction: down the river plain to the south goes the track to the Mongolian border at Naushki, whereas eastwards out of the valleys and up onto the plateau runs the line to Vladivostok (and also to Pyongyang, North Korea) and, branching off the Vladivostok line, the line to Harbin, where I'm headed. I climb the footbridge and look down on the pair of trains. Smoke belches from the boilers in each of the carriages, and railway workers swarm around them with supplies of coal, mail and food. I give the driver a wave as I head back. He gives me a thumbs up, but looks at me like I might be a bit mad. Back at carriage 4 there are a few enterprising vendors on foot selling the local fish from the lake.They are displayed for inspection, hung on a big hook, so you can select the most appetising one. The fish are a delicacy, but a very smelly one.

Inside our carriage there are now far better smells. Rima has been making meat dumplings, and now she's cooking them on a shovel in the samovar fire. She offers me one to try, and once I work out how to fit it into my mouth without creating a mess, it tastes delicious. The train will reach the Chinese border in about 24 hours, so tonight is probably going to be my last Russian dinner. I'm thinking of having Valerie's speciality dish, a pork escalope served with fried potatoes and tasteful garnish. Food on the train so far has been pretty good. Other than an absence of fresh bread, if you're not too fussy there is nearly everything you could want here, and it's not too expensive. I'm not sure it would make a healthy diet in the long term, but for a week it's fine.

So much for a good night's sleep. The train has frozen brakes, and every time it slows down my carriage lurches backwards and forwards. At 03.39 I'm actually thrown out of my bed. I don't think we have collided with anything – just a huge wobble and then a jolt. Everything not tied down flies into the air. The good news is that my stash of booze is undamaged, the bad news that my reading glasses are broken. If this wasn't a big enough event for one night, I also have to get up before each stop to reseal my window. It's a high-maintenance activity, but well worth it, as the ambient internal temperature is a stifling 29°C.

Raising the insulated roller blind, I'm greeted by yet another unfamiliar landscape. We have been slowly climbing for several hours, and the view is now of a vast uninhabited tundra plain and in the distance the Great Khingan mountain range. We have reached Outer Manchuria. In the night we have passed through a rail junction at Chita. Here the trains to Vladivostok continue eastwards, and those going to the Chinese border at Manzhouli turn south. I'm in a part of Siberia that I have never travelled in before and this adds a dimension of excitement and discovery.

Valerie has taken to passing me notes with mostly helpful things scribbled on them. He knows that after today I'm going to be without his personal translation service, as the restaurant carriage will not be crossing the border. His first note of the day has just a number on it: 31. Except that there is a tiny minus sign in front of it. This ties in with my earlier bathroom experience, in that the toilet has frozen solid. Even the modern Russian carriages need hot water to keep the pressurised systems from freezing. The problem is that the toilet is the opposite end of the carriage from the samovar, and as I'm the only passenger, the hot water is sitting too long in the pipes and so freezing up. Sergei has called out the engineer from wherever he lives on the train.

A long stop at Borzya reveals that we are carrying a lot of mail but few passengers; on this leg of the journey the RZD staff and security greatly outnumber travellers. The town here was originally established to move military equipment into eastern Mongolia during the Japanese invasion in 1939, and today most of the factories and buildings are derelict. It looks like a place without a purpose in today's world. I climb down onto the platform, which is at ground level and very narrow – and I am seriously startled when a freight train passes by just inches from my face. You really have to have your wits about yourself at some of these stations; with a covering of snow, it would be too easy to confuse the platform with the tracks. The noise of the passing train is deafening and repetitive as each of the oil wagons clanks past.

Up here on the plateau it's much drier, and my throat and eyes are becoming sore. I have started to cough as the freezing dry air is removing any moisture from my lungs. In the Himalayas climbers call this a Khumbu cough. What little moisture there is in my breath freezes in my beard, which I quite like as it makes me feel like a polar explorer. The local traders here have got used to life in such an inhospitable place. They move between platforms to sell door-to-door to passengers, their goods pulled around on purpose-built sledges. The offerings here look surprisingly gourmet to me; local honey, coffee beans, fresh bread and dried fish are all on sale.

We will be at the Chinese border in a few hours. A phrase like 'a few hours' now seems perfectly acceptable on a journey like this. If someone asked you how long a journey in Europe was going to take, you might answer with a definitive number of hours and minutes, but after nearly a week on this train 'a few hours' is just a period of time that you use to eat or read, not something that needs any active consideration. I use the time to go and say goodbye to Valerie and the Russians who won't be coming with us. Soon the train will split in two and the 'Russian zone', made up of the restaurant and a couple of kupe sleeper carriages, will be left behind. People are busy reorganising luggage and supplies around where the split will take place and I too had better make sure I'm in the right part of the train when that happens. I shall feel sad to see Valerie and the team go; I've met many helpful people on trains all over the world, but none that have been so kind. We exchange small gifts, and before I leave I ask Valerie if he minds if I take his photograph. He agrees, but insists on changing into his full uniform and will only pose very formally for me behind the bar. He explains that he doesn't want to smile as he is hiding his gold fillings. I get a bit emotional when I say goodbye. I have only known him for a week, but he has treated me like an extended member of his family. I, like so many travellers, have almost invariably found the Russians to be friendly, and this train crew has been a wonderful example.

Chapter Nine:
Escape from Zabaikalsk

As we pull into the Russian frontier station at Zabai-kalsk, Sergei appears in the corridor and insists that I must leave the train immediately and go inside the station. No questions, no time to explain. Get off now! I have no idea why. I literally just grab my day bag with my essentials and do as I'm told, not at all clear on how this is going to work. The inside of the building is laid out more like an airport than a conventional station, and with nothing to do I sit down on an uncomfortable plastic chair in a large empty waiting room. I wish I had picked up my coat. Then the blood in my veins runs cold. Through the window I spot the Vostok pulling away. It's finally happened. I am now officially separated from my luggage, which is on a train headed to an unknown destination. Be cool, I tell myself, this must just be how things work here. There is no one to ask. I'm alone.

I wait for a while and then wait for a while more. I decide that nothing's going to happen in a hurry here, and that I have some time to explore the rest of the station. Down the corridor there is an office manned by some immigration people, but all they seem to be interested in at present is their lunch. They won't talk to me, and wave me back to the waiting room. My thought is that this might be the sort of frontier that you walk through with your paperwork, but there is no obvious route through the glass partitions. I seem to be trapped in Mother Russia.

A handful of passengers drift in, I don't know where they have come from. They're Chinese. I do my best to communicate with them in international sign language and get absolutely nowhere. Then comes a man's voice behind me, first speaking Mandarin and then switching to a language I recognise: clear and well-pronounced English. I'm thrown to discover that he's neither Chinese or English, though. His name is Robert and he turns out to be Swiss. He introduces me to his travelling companion, Chris. Not only does Robert speak Mandarin, but Chris speaks Russian. What a special power to have in these parts. Imagine what they must be able to do with skills like that as a double act. Superheroes! I quickly forget their real names, as I think of Robert as Batman and Chris as Spiderman. Whilst Batman has been talking to the Chinese, Spiderman has been on a close target recce of the rest of the station and found a ticket counter. The Chinese apparently say we will be here for several hours, and Chris has also found a café of sorts. The good news is the train is coming back, because it's having its bogies changed for the narrower Chinese gauge. I had forgotten all about the need for this. It would have been good if Sergei had mentioned it to me before.

The café is a strange place. Its delicacies are part-Russian, part-Chinese. We drink Russian beerand eat Manchurian pasties. These are filled with an unexpected combination of hot dog sausageand mashed potato. The novelty is great when you've been living on the limited train menu for a week. A couple of hours pass quickly and with a bit too much beer for passengers about to cross one of the tougher borders in the world. It turns out that my superhero friends have been on the train since Irkutsk, drinking and dining in the same restaurant carriage as me, but on a completely different time zone from mine. I feel totally relaxed in their company, protected by their special powers. An announcement over the public address system signals that our train is ready for boarding. I'm confused by this, as we have not done any immigration checks here, but I'm not going to hang about to find out why. I try to keep up with Batman and Spiderman as we find a way back to the platform. They are in a carriage at the other end of the train, so reluctantly I say goodbye to them and hope I see them once we are over the border.

Sergei is waiting for me at carriage 4 and he seems keen to have me back in his carriage without delay. I find this new hurry-up-and-wait regime tedious, to say the least, but once again I do as instructed and return to my compartment, where a small pile of paperwork has appeared on my table. But there is something else different. Sergei has put on his full-dress uniform. He is also now wearing strong aftershave, a Russian version of Brut 33 or Hi Karate. What sort of a border is this going to be?

In the finest traditions of international rail travel, we first need to deal with the police, customs and immigration of the country we are leaving. The officials who have been eating a long lunch of noodles now emerge on the platform and target each carriage in small groups. With only half a dozen passengers, the officials outnumber us three to one. Sergei's encouragements have apparently been so I can complete the Russian forms before these people arrive. He doesn't know that I'm a speed formfiller, and that I know all my passport details from memory. The Russian officer who visits me takes a lot of time examining my passport and then my visa. She confers with a colleague and they talk about me in the corridor. Eventually one of them comes in and points at the photo page. 'Woodward?' she says, and then 'Wrong date.'

Trying to figure out what she means, at first I think that my visa dates might be wrong. Then she shows me my passport. She is pointing to my 'valid until' date. 'Not possible,' she adds. Oh dear. This is the same travel document and biometric visa that I have managed to enter the Russian Federation with – but now it would seem I'm not able to leave. I wonder how many European passports they see on this frontier – probably not many – but then another thought occurs. My previous passport was renewed before its expiry date, as I had run out of space with all the visas. When you renew early, you get extra validity beyond the standard ten years on the new document. How am I going to explain that using my 'point at it' book and Russian dating translator app? Sergei and Rima are nowhere to be seen, so I speak slowly and slightly loudly. The officers look at each other like I'm talking gibberish, and head off to seek advice on how to handle the man with a counterfeit passport in carriage 4. Reinforcements arrive, and the best English speaker in the unit translates. They look at me like it can't be true, but eventually concede that it might be possible. I'm left a marked man, but the good news is that it looks like I'm going to able to leave.

Five hours after we've arrived at Zabaikalsk, the train trundles out of the station, complete with its new narrower-gauge bogies. It's getting dark and I turn the lights out so I can see better outside, to find out what happens where Russia meets China. In the distance are the colourful bright lights of Manchzhuriya (Manzhouli): big business hotels, casinos and concrete follies. The Chinese like to make a statement with their borders. As my eyes adjust I notice the cameras. Hundreds of them, pointing in all directions. Cameras looking at cameras. Even cameras angled to look directly into the carriages of our train. Soldiers are standing to attention in little sentry boxes. Then no buildings; just fences, more cameras and searchlights. This must be no man's land. At this moment I get to witness one of the funniest sights that I have ever seen on an international border. From the Chinese side, a train slowly approaches pulling a single carriage full of officials. It's the Keystone Cops. But I'm careful not to laugh – that's rule number 8: always treat border officials with the utmost respect. They hop down from their carriage and board our train. The first one I meet seems pleased to see me. Once he finds out where I'm from he welcomes me to China and takes away my passport. Everything goes smoothly from this point on, and other than a thorough search of my bag, I seem to be quickly accepted as suitable for entry. There is a bit of culture shock here, as the

Chinese officials seem to smile a lot compared to those on the other side of the frontier. In reality I don't think it makes them any more or less friendly; it's just the different norms and protocols in communicating.

The sound of slamming doors, and our carriage becomes silent again. We move off from our halt in no man's land at a snail's pace. As we get closer to the station, Manchzhuriya looks like it might be a bit of a party town for local businessmen with a taste for gambling and karaoke. But I'm unable to sample the nightlife as I'm a captive of the international platform in the station. The architecture is unfamiliar to me. There is absolutely nothing standing on the platform itself. Modern electronic display boards are mounted overhead, and the place is devoid of both human and animal life. There are no shops or even vending machine. Nothing is on sale. But now that we're over the border Sergei seems to be more talkative again. His news is mixed, though; we are going to be here for several hours, but I can get off the train, and there is a station building.

As there is now no power on board, rather than waiting in the darkness of my compartment I follow him down the platform and up the steps of the monolithic station building. I need to sell the roubles that will be useless for the rest of my journey, and Sergei says there is a place to do this upstairs. The station has been built to cope with huge numbers of passengers who have yet to materialise. It is set up like an airport, and I have to do the equivalent of leaving the arrivals area and clearing security to get back into departures. Here a few families mill around between small shops mostly selling expensive bottles of domestically produced brandy and cigarettes. Beside one of the shops are a couple of people with a desk made out of some cardboard boxes. On top of the boxes is a big office calculator, the kind that prints out computations on a roll of paper, and a banknote counter. One look at them and I know they are black market currency traders: one look at me and they know I have some money to exchange. My roubles are inspected, and exchanged for a pile of yuan. There are no published rates to consult and I have the choice of doing the deal or walking away. It turns out to be an instructive experience for me. First, not to trust black market currency traders, and secondly not to be pointlessly angry at myself when I realise I have been ripped off by their exchange rate. This is a useful reminder to myself to be in better control of situations like this on the street, and I consider the tuition fee well spent. In these parts there are a few well practised traveller scams; most revolve around art shows, tea ceremonies and accusations of paying with a fake note. This experience has been like a tetanus shot in the behind, and my immune system is now on full alert again.

The only edible items on sale in the station are cartons of dried noodles. As I can't see the attraction of hanging around in here, I decide that I would rather be back in the comfort of my own compartment on the Vostok, even without power. But I can't get back on the train without Sergei, as he has locked up the carriage. I wait for him as he does his shopping and then we walk back together. Not only is there no electricity on board the train, but there's no hot water either, so no noodles. The tastiest looking items in my ration bag not requiring hot water are a tin of Russian corned beef (or the nearest meat equivalent) and some crackers. But then I remember that I have the unopened parcel from the Edinburgh Explorers Club. With some excitement I remove the string and tear open the brown paper. Several items fall out onto my lap, including a miniature bottle of 10-year-old Scotch whisky, a bar of Kendal Mint Cake, a pot of Gentleman's Relish and a packet of shortbread. An unexpected feast!

One of the main tricks to enjoying long-range rail adventure is that you just have to convince your mind that you don't care how long you're waiting for. Once you have achieved this state you can sit back, read, write and smile, and before you know it you're on the move again. The border crossing today has taken more than 11 hours, and I've managed to keep smiling for most of the day. I give myself a little pat on the back and treat myself to tot of whisky.

With dawn comes my final day on the Vostok. The carriage has filled up with a few Chinese passengers and we are now bound for Harbin. It's good to have some company in the carriage, but they are mostly noisy and not very engaging to a farang (foreigner) like me. On my trip to the samovar I meet the short but very fit-looking man who now lives next door. He has tied-back shoulder-length grey hair and is as skinny as a bicycle. He bows deeply when he sees me, his hands clasped together in front of him. I return a little bow whilst maintaining eye contact. He then makes the sort of sound you hear in a martial arts dojo: 'Ouoooooooos.' I make a mental note to treat him with extra respect, just in case he decides to start chopping up the carriage with his bare hands later on.

Manchuria is a frozen land of half-built tower blocks, oil wells, and concrete factories rapidly advancing on the ancient farmland. There is a distinct smog in the air, the haze of dust and industrial pollution. Harbin is the only scheduled stop in the timetable today, at lunchtime Beijing time. China runs on a single time zone, so with the adjustment made at the border, my watch will stay at GMT -8 for the rest of my journey. The origin of the name Harbin is a Manchu word meaning 'a place for drying fishing nets'. It sounds slightly primitive, but today this is the biggest city in north-eastern China, best known perhaps for its winter ice festival, when huge ice sculptures are decorated with bright lights. Quite why I have not planned to stop here I can't remember, but I must have had my eye on the limited window of dates available for getting the permit for Tibet. I need to get to Beijing soon, to make sure that all my paperwork is in order.

Nothing interesting or ice-related is visible from the modern and sterile station platform at Harbin. But on a trainspotting-related note, there is now a raised high-speed line running continuously alongside our tracks, and on it Chinese high-speed G trains flick past us in the blink of an eye. Trillions of yuan have been spent on the new network, and journeys that once took days in China now take hours. Two railway worlds now exist, and here the new stands next to the old. Separated by just a platform, old-fashioned sleeper trains like the Vostok sit alongside the bullet-shaped vision of the future. We have 40 minutes here, so I pull my jacket on and take a stroll to see how the composition of our train has changed.

The platform is covered overhead, so there is no snow on it and I'm up front with the locomotive in just a couple of minutes. As I admire the strange-looking Chinese locomotive for the first time I hear shouting behind me and then a whistle. Turning back to see what is causing the commotion, I discover that it's me. The guard on the platform doesn't seem very pleased to see me. He doesn't think I should be free to roam on his platform, let alone in the vicinity of the engine. There are obviously no trainspotters amongst the five million people who live in the city. Using sign language to try and explain, I point my camera at the train and pretend to be interested in the detailed engineering of the locomotive. I complete the charade to Lionel Blair standards and I'm permitted to go about my business. On the way back, I pass the newly added Chinese restaurant car and peer in through its grimy windows. There seems to be little activity – just a few guards drinking tea. At least I know where it is now, but rather strangely I decide that I would prefer to eat some Russian instant noodles for lunch today. They are delicious. So delicious in fact that I also decide to have some for dinner. What's going on? A week in Siberia and I have become a noodle addict. Once the noodlefest is over I pack my bags and organise my belongings, as tomorrow morning we will be arriving in Beijing.

At 5 am I get a knock on my compartment door. It's Rima, and she just says one word to me – 'Peking!' It's a Phileas Fogg moment; I wish I had a top hat and frock coat. I wish Rima and Sergei well; they have been the most friendly and helpful provodniki that I have ever met, and I am sure I will miss them as I move to the Chinese way of life on the rails. I get my kit onto the platform, but after a week in my compartment, I'm worried I might leave something important behind, so I go back to check twice before I finally leave the now familiar comfort of the train for the platform.Turning down the offers of several porters, I wheel my bags down into the cavernous underpass that connects the platforms of Beijing's central station with its concourse. It's busy, but at this time of the day the crowds are manageable. Outside I'm confronted by weird weather; visibility is just a few feet, as a dense blanket of smog covers the city. Eventually finding a taxi that isn't in the pay of a tout, I am driven out onto the ring road; my driver can probably see more of the road on his satnav than through the windscreen this morning. Ground radar would be a helpful optional extra in a car in this city. When we reach my hotel I'm braced for a rip-off fare. But how big a rip-off will it be? A little rip-off that you tolerate on arriving in any new city, or a massive rip-off that you have to fight, and threaten to call the police? I have the exchange rate loaded into my phone and my calculator at the ready. He points at the meter. Have I got it wrong? Decimal places can be a minefield of misunderstanding. But no, it's just 25 yuan, around £3. Happy days. I now have some time to rest and relax in the city before I get ready to undertake my journey to Tibet on the highest railway in the world.

Chapter Ten:
The Scorpion King

Untangling myself from the duvet, I eventually locate an edge of my strange new bed, then the desk, and finally the button that automatically opens the curtains. Outside, office workers in nearby modern skyscrapers stare back at me across the misty boulevard. They're dressed in suits, though, and I'm just wearing a pair of pants. Beijing. I'm in Beijing.

I have been in bed for over 12 hours, and feel really well rested for the first time in a couple of weeks. Having missed breakfast, I make some coffee and spend a couple of hours repacking my bags and arranging some laundry. Looking at the hotel laundry price list, it might be cheaper to just buy new clothes, but I'm doubtful if the local fashions would suit me as well as they might Michael Portillo. A quiet knock at the door to my room, and then a louder one. It's the concierge with a courier delivery. It'll be some tickets. I haven't had time to worry about them not arriving in time for my departure, proof that I'm living in the moment.

Inside the cardboard envelope are the train tickets from a local agent for my train to Lhasa. But I haven't been sent an onward ticket, just an inbound one. So it takes a few email exchanges with Moscow to work out that more than one agent has been used, the other one being based in Lhasa. For now, I have just a one-way ticket and a photocopy of my Tibet permit. On examining the little blue piece of paper, I can see no English written on it, so I have to assume it is what I'm told it is. It has no less than four big red ink stamps on it, each with a star and a lot of Chinese characters. Let's hope it's not a lottery ticket or an insurance policy. It's clearly going to get inspected before I'm allowed to board the train, so I can only hope that a photocopy will be sufficient. My train ticket to 'Lasa' looks okay, other than it has actually been issued to a 'Mr Matthew'. Whilst this would not work back home, in Chinese there is often some confusion around western family names. I'm to be in carriage 5, berth 14. I hope this is an auspicious carriage and berth allocation.

With my chores complete, I have time for a walk to a nearby shopping centre infamous for selling almost entirely counterfeit goods. Known as the

Silk Market, it became a political hot potato in the run-up to the 2008 Olympic Games. It was pulled down to show China's hardening attitude to copyright and patent infringement – and then rebuilt as soon as the games were over, but much bigger. It's a den of thieves behind the curtained doorway. On the third floor I take a seat at a foot massage parlour and use this as place to watch the interactions between confused farangs and aggressive traders. Then it's my turn; having agreed a price for a foot massage, I realise too late that this is only the start of the negotiation. The manageress offers a range of bolt-on special treatments, wraps and lotions, each with a price. After several attempts to upsell they give up and stick to what I have asked for. Opposite is a tailor's shop, and in the window a beaming picture of George Bush Senior. He gets everywhere; I see him in shops right across South East Asia. I only wonder what he does with all those suits.

At the top of the escalator to the fourth floor, hundreds of little stores are selling watches. No dodgy men with a briefcase asking if anyone wants to buy a Rolex. Instead, shopfront after shopfront offering watches of every conceivable brand. Most have salesmen outside shouting and grabbing shoppers. I'm therefore attracted to one that seems to have no hustlers, and no interest in me. Inside a lady eyes me up and says 'You wan' watch?'. 'Just looking,' I tell her. 'Looking is free,' she says, as if in other places I would be charged extra for this. I'm saddened that such a trade is possible. Thinking of a way of ending my visit without loss of face, I ask if she has a specific watch that is quite rare in the real world. Totally unfazed, she pulls out a box stuffed full of the particular model I have asked for. I feign interest for a respectable amount of time and then say, 'Bye bye,' words that seem to be understood around the world. As I head for the escalator she shouts at me down the corridor, her price going down, until finally she shouts words that make me blush. What a depressing place – a shopping centre for tourists to buy imitation items to take home. There are no Chinese people shopping here.

Modern-day Beijing is full of paradox, both physical and cultural. Trendy bars are taking over the ancient hutongs (alleyways), set beneath the sky-high buildings of the metropolis. Shops running tea ceremony scams sit next to restaurants serving world-class cuisine with tea so good it gets its own menu. I have to face the fact that many people I encounter are after my money, and as a traveller I'm fair game. But even so, after a day of dodging fictitious art sales, being short-changed and being shouted at I'm at a bit of a low ebb. Being brutal in negotiation can sometimes be the Chinese way, but when did people just stop caring about strangers? The rapid and exponential growth of this city must breed aggression and a desire for wealth that is all-consuming.

Just when I think everyone is against me, I find kindness in an unexpected quarter. Wangfujing is a pedestrianised street near the centre of the city, famous for the exotic snacks sold by the vendors in its side streets. Trying to take arty photographs of freshly cooked worms isn't working out very well; I can't hold the worm and photograph it at the same time. I sense that taking a photograph of anyone here is also probably going to mean paying for the privilege, so I hang back and take snaps from a respectable distance. But I have been rumbled, and the body of a man obscures my viewfinder. He's the bug chef, the Scorpion King. Dressed in white overalls, wellington boots and a baseball cap, he smiles and invites me over to his nearby stall. Here, trays of scorpions, worms, and grubs are lined up neatly in white food-grade plastic trays. To one side there are also little samples on sticks, ready to taste. I'm not brave enough to try the scorpion, so he offers me a worm-based dish, and I decide I'm going to give it a go. It has a strange taste, and an unexpected kick. If I ate it every day I might even get used to it. The Scorpion King seems impressed and insists I try one of his finest bugs. This is a big mistake. It tastes truly vile and I can't get bits out of my mouth without causing a scene, so I have to swallow it. Once I have recovered, he insists that he takes my photograph posing with a basket of little critters on kebab sticks. Nearby vendors scowl at us, but he keeps smiling. He must have a higher goal in life than his competitors. I try to pay him, but he refuses to take my money. Instead he gives me a warm nod and a thumbs-up sign, as if to say 'well done' for challenging my culinary comfort zone.

Back at the downstairs bar in my hotel, the peanuts are free and the beer is very cold. It's a classy place, and it quickly fills up with wealthy-looking expats. Smoking is perfectly normal in here, and cigars are the weapon of choice. Large, fat and Cuban. It's a rare chance, and a bit of a relief, for me to speak to people in my own language; after a couple of weeks on the rails, I'm happy to talk to anyone and everyone. On one side of the bar are a couple of businessmen selling property, and on the other a South African couple on their honeymoon. You could get used to this place if it wasn't for the prices. As the evening wears on the lights get dimmer and the band gets louder, but all good things have to come to an end, so I make my excuses and retire before late becomes early. Tomorrow I will be taking the train across China and upward to the Tibetan Plateau.

Chapter Eleven:
The Z21 to Lhasa

My taxi has been stuck in an afternoon traffic jam
on the Beijing ring road for more than an hour, but
I'm zoned out in pre-travel meditation in the back
seat. The drivers in this city seem reasonably well
behaved, and we nudge forward ever closer to
Beijing West railway station without any need for the
horn. The final hurdle is the spiral ramp that takes
taxis up to the concourse level of the station. It's a
bit of a bun fight to get to the head of the queue of
passengers outside the station, but once my tickets
have been checked, I'm in. I like to think of railway
stations as places where relatives can wave off
departing friends and relatives, but not here; the
only people allowed into the station are passengers
travelling today. Next is the security check;
unfortunately there is something magnetic and
preordained about me and x-ray machines – however

carefully I load my bags onto the belt, I seem to get stuck on the belt and nearly enter the guts of the machine itself. Today it's another near miss. Straightening my clothing as if that's quite normal where I come from, I stroll through the scanner intended for humans.

In front of me in the huge open concourse is a departure board the size of a squash court. It flashes and pulsates in red and green characters in the manner of an early game of space invaders. I spot occasional words of English before they're shot down and replaced with Chinese characters. But eventually I spot it, the Z21, departing at 20.10, destination 'Lasa': Waiting Room Number 6. The railway waiting room has been re-engineered in a unique way in China. It roughly equates to a gate at an airport, except that multiple trains board from each room and passengers intermingle freely. A waiting room sounds like a calm and relaxing place where you might be able to sit back, read and discuss the cricket results with a fellow passenger. But this is Beijing West, where whole regiments of passengers with boxes of provisions prepare to travel. Whilst there are a few seats in the room, for most it's not a waiting room at all, but a standing and shouting room. At one side of the room is a roped-off seating area, where a uniform guard looks at my ticket and decides she doesn't like it. My reservation is in a soft class four-berth compartment, which equates to first class in Russia, but she doesn't consider me to have the credentials of a VIP suitable for one of her seats. So now, what next? At the far end of the waiting room are four gates, each with a list of trains due to depart. I head for one of them. The only snag is that between me and the right one are hundreds if not thousands of travellers with the same plan. The trick is timing your pushing to arrive at the front of the teeming mass at the right moment. I get it wrong, and sheepishly show my ticket to the inspector who is still boarding an earlier train. He directs me to wait at the naughty seat by his side, thankfully protecting me from the jostling crowd. Pole position. This is the Chinese railway equivalent of 'Speedy Boarding'.

At this station, the number of the place where you wait for your train has no bearing on the number of your platform; you might wait in room number 1, go through ticket check number 4 and then board on platform 9. My train isn't a normal one, in the sense that it is one of just a very few with international or controlled domestic destinations. Once boarding commences at the gate, I pull out the photocopy of my Tibet permit and hand it to the inspector, together with my ticket. My papers seem to be in order, and he lets me pass. The pressure of the crowd behind me forces me onward and into the corridor. Descending the long concrete staircase from the bridge while balancing my bags as best as I can, I eventually reach the platform. Passengers dart past me on both sides. Why are they in such a hurry? Surely everyone has a seat reservation of some sort? Our train is so long that I can't see either end; the carriages just reach a vanishing point. On the platform I'm directed forwards, and find carriage 5 where the attendants are ready to recheck my ticket and make sure I'm on the manifest.

My soft class carriage is made up of eight four-berth compartments, and I have an upper berth in a compartment towards the middle. The upper berth is a bit of a disaster, but these trains are always full and I will just have to make the best of it. I only wish I had completed a mountain climbing refresher course before setting out, as I don't yet have the technique required. The first step seems far too low, and there is no rope to pull on to get up and onto the bunk. So I develop a technique that involves perching on both upper bunks with my knees, like parallel bars. I think this scares a girl called Jenny in the other upper bunk, as she is not sure of my intentions. My other immediate concern is how four passengers will be able to fit all our luggage in, but with a bit of experimentation we eventually manage it. As my big bag is soft-sided, it can be squeezed into the roof space, which is quite deep in this carriage. The trick is to ensure you won't need to get anything out of it during the journey, and all the kit I will need access to is already in my daypack.

Below are a young city couple. He introduces himself as Audi, and his partner Rachel. Audi seems like an odd English name, but he insists it is spelled 'like the car'. Jenny helps. His name is Andy. My first reaction is that judging by the boisterous crowd in the waiting room I've been lucky; I sense that up here in soft class the passengers are largely young aspiring Chinese professionals getting away on a short holiday to an exotic destination.

Right on time, music is played on the platform, the guards salute the train and coloured lights flash. We trundle out of the station and pick up speed as we pass through the outer suburbs of Beijing. The attendant stops by and collects tickets, replacing them with a special card to prove that we are legitimate passengers on the train. Mine is a gold one, and I wonder if it might have special on-board benefits. An executive washroom would be nice.

Whilst my compartment mates unpack and arrange their supplies, I take a moment to conduct a close target recce of my new surroundings. The good news is that this carriage is directly attached to the restaurant carriage, so there will be no lengthy walks. The design of the interior is slightly different from the everyday Chinese sleeper train; at one end is a large glass panel, behind which are rows of glowing lights and dials. I have never been in a modern submarine, but imagine that this is what the reactor room would look like. This is where the environment is carefully controlled, including the oxygen levels. I glance at each of the dials like I know what I'm looking at. I'm sure green lights are better than red ones, but a few are flashing red. Opposite the glass panel is a samovar. It's a fully fitted one, not like the exposed polished boilers that you find on Russian trains. It's already very popular this evening, and there is an orderly a queue of passengers waiting to make their instant noodles. Chinese noodles are considerably more sophisticated than those that are sold in Europe. Inside the carton are a series of packets that need to be added in just the right order with precision timing. Some patience is required, and you can't just dive in like a ravenous student back from the pub on a Friday night. Down the other end of the corridor is an open-plan washroom area with several sinks. I'm pleased I remembered to put my flip-flops in my daypack, as this is very much a wet environment. The area is part-flooded and seems multi-purpose. For some it's vegetable preparation, for others it's waste disposal. Next door to this place are a pair of toilets, one western, and one squatter: a hole in the floor of the carriage and a shower attachment that many call a 'bum gun'.

Back in the compartment I perch on the end of Andy's berth. There is a certain etiquette to this. In the daytime it is normal protocol that the lower berths are used as seats for all four passengers, but the owner of those berths can call shotgun in the evening when they want to go to bed. Your options then are to retire to the upper berth or perch on one of the little pull-down seats in the corridor. This evening the table and lower beds have limited room for people, as they are covered in personal belongings, mainly plastic bags filled with food.

Andy looks keen to settle in for the night, so I take my leave and head for the restaurant, not forgetting my newly issued gold card. The carriage is busy, a lively mix of off-duty police and slightly drunk shouty passengers. It has beer of sorts, Chinese Budweiser, for 10 RMB, around £1. The bottles are not chilled, though, just pulled out of a cardboard case stacked on the floor next to the kitchen. But warm beer is probably a blessing in disguise, as I should not be drinking tonight. I started taking my diamox pills this morning and I need to get properly hydrated to minimise the effects of altitude. We are currently only 40m above sea level, but tomorrow night we will be crossing more than one mountain pass of over 4000m. I allow myself just one beer to celebrate having Beijing West behind me and to observe the dining habits of my fellow passengers. We make a short stop at Shijiazhuang late in the evening, and I use this as a marker that it's time for me to get some rest.

Back in carriage 5 everything is very quiet, and I attempt to brush my teeth using a bottle of mineral water without getting too wet or contaminated in the process. Sounds of coughing and snoring now emanate from compartments up and down the corridor. My compartment is in darkness and I feel my way around as my eyes adjust. I'd like to say that I climbed into bed with the grace and style of a stealthy ninja. Instead I fall off the first rung of the ladder and land on Rachel's berth. I don't actually land on her, but she jumps up in bed all the same. Andy puts the lights on and, apologies made, I make a second attempt at the climb, this time successfully, under the scrutiny of my cabin mates. To give them credit, they might have cursed me in their own language, but they are polite about it to me. With the lights turned off once again, I settle in for the night. Upper berths can be quite nice places once you are in them, and as long as you don't fall out. They are a bit more private, and on some trains wider than the lower bunk, which has to convert into a seat during the day. Up top, my watch provides a soft glow, enough to see the light controls at one end of my bed, and next to them a place to plug in an oxygen mask. A sign of what might be to come.

Chapter Twelve:
Heaven and Hell in Zhongwei

I am up well before we reach Zhongwei at 07.10 the following morning. In fact, I've been up for most of the night, feeling pretty miserable. In the early hours I go into a negative thought spiral. I like to think that one of my most precious skills on the rails is remaining positive in the face of adversity. But the rapidly deteriorating state of the carriage really gets to me. The toilets have become seriously bad so quickly that in a weak moment I nearly wish that I'm not on the train. Then just to push me over the edge, I return to our compartment where there is now an overpowering stench of stale urine. I lie in my berth desperately trying to understand this. Is the toilet plumbed into the aircon of the carriage? Or have my cabin mates just been caught short and relieved themselves on the floor? Half an hour's deep thought on how to raise the subject of bathroom etiquette with my cabin mates, and I come up with something that I decide might be more plausible. They must have been snacking on Durian fruit, also known throughout much of Asia simply as 'stink fruit'. It smells so bad that it is banned from public transport in much of South East Asia.

The air on board is very dry and I sleep in short bursts, waking with a dry mouth and eyes. A child in the compartment next door has been kicking the dividing wall and screaming through most of the night. But my boss used to say to me that 'the darkest moment of the night is just before dawn', and indeed I feel considerably better just after the sun has risen, as we pull into Zhongwei. I pull myself together and try to embrace all that's going on around me: the man next door singing at the top of his voice, the lady with the trolley passing by every few minutes shouting what I guess is the Chinese for 'breakfast', the endless phone and text ringtones, even the wet end of the carriage. I tell myself to just suck it all in. It's all part of the adventure.

Practising some positive mental attitude techniques, I remind myself what is good about the train. This is an authentic traditional long-distance Chinese Z train, a style of travel that is slowly being killed off as high-speed services connect nearly every province of the country. On these trains you get to experience real life with real people. The carriage itself has an excellent air conditioning system, and for the first time on this whole adventure I feel it is the right temperature on board. The ride is incredibly smooth; at times you barely feel the movement. If I had a 50 pence piece I could probably balance it on its side on the table – if the table weren't covered in fruit peelings, Chinese herbal medicines and empty bottles of cheap beer.

Jenny leaves the train later that morning and no one takes her place. She will probably be telling her family all about a night sharing a compartment with a crazy foreigner. As soon as she has gone we eye up the extra space in the compartment and spread out a bit more. Rachel is preparing lunch, which consists of noodles, strange fruit and various medicines wrapped in small parcels of newspaper. She and Andy offer me a place at their table and various things to eat, but I seem to have lost my appetite. Andy insists that I drink the contents of a small glass vial with a little straw. The liquid is muddy brown, and I can only hope that no endangered species have been involved in producing it. He says it's for my health, but I'm somewhat doubtful. Sucking it up, I find it tastes sweet and thankfully of nothing else. Smiles all round when I finish it, but then he hands me another one, and I don't like to refuse in case I cause offence.

On the platform at Lanzhou there is plenty of food on sale, mostly from well-stocked wooden carts. One woman is selling tasty-looking flatbreads stuffed with fried chicken, but I decide not risk it; a stomach upset at altitude would be seriously debilitating. Instead I buy some nectarines and hang out with the locals, who are all very friendly. They insist on having their photo taken with me. I want to leave a good impression of my nationality, as the single British representative travelling on the train in this remote part of China. I look Lanzhou up on the map; it's in Gansu Province.

The landscape outside the train is unfamiliar to me. Steep bare mountains, lush flood plains and salt lakes as far as the eye can see. Big birds of prey cruise overhead. I spend a couple of hours in the afternoon sitting in the restaurant carriage drinking tea. It's not PG Tips, but a big jar filled with green leaves floating on top of freshly boiled water. I stir it with a long spoon and relax. Everything starts to feel good again.

I'm learning that on this journey it's best to catch some sleep whenever you can. Rest is a precious commodity in the acclimatisation game. and the altitude at tea time is already around 2000 metres. I can check this whenever I like, as the height of each stop is printed on an information sheet at the end of the carriage as well on the digital read-out of the nuclear reactor panel. I feel fine now, but tonight we will be climbing much higher, reaching our highest point just before dawn. The train will then actually descend a bit before we arrive in Lhasa.

The big stop of the evening is a place called Golmud, which we reach at 22.30. There don't seem to be many passengers joining or leaving us here, but there is much shunting going on. This is where they swap the engines for the more specialised high-altitude locomotives. Our arrival here means that we are now in Qinghai Province, on the edge of the Tibetan Plateau, if not yet quite in the Tibet Autonomous Prefecture. Inside our dark compartment there is a strange new noise. It sounds like someone has accidentally switched on the radio, but all that is coming out of the speaker in the ceiling is white noise. I find my head torch and have a look round. I can't find a switch to adjust the radio, but as I move around I realise the source of the noise is actually much closer to my head, and it's more of a whooshing noise. Oxygen-enriched air is now being pumped in to each of the mask connectors, one per berth.

The night is long, and at times rather rough. I lie in my berth panting and suffering from periodic breathing. I awake several times in a panic. A further altitude-related complication are the side effects of taking diamox. I am sure that without the drug I would be feeling much worse, but it makes me want to pee more, so several times in the night I have to negotiate my way down from my upper bunk and through the wet end of the carriage. Whilst I'm getting better at negotiating the drop down from and the climb back into my bed, I'm finding that it requires seemingly large amounts of motivation and effort to move.

When I wake at around 5 am my ears are popping a lot and my body is very hot. The train seems not to be able to support air conditioning and an enriched air supply at the same time. As it's impossible to sleep, I get up and escape the hot dark smelly pit that our compartment has become. In the comparative coolness of the corridor I pull down a little seat and perch by the window, waiting for the first light of a Tibetan dawn.

Other than a mild headache and heavy breathing, I feel fine. A cup of hot sweet tea gives me the energy to go for a wander down the corridor to consult the altimeter: 4950 metres. I am as high as I was at school camp on Mount Kilimanjaro, but without having had any time for my body to acclimatise from the near-sea level of Beijing. And we're still climbing. I have read somewhere that the extra oxygen-enriched air being pumped in will keep our carriage at an equivalent altitude of around 2000 metres, rather like a jet plane. But the carriage isn't pressurised like a plane, so I'm not sure how this can be possible.

As the sun creeps above the mountainous skyline I have my first view of the plains of frozen lakes punctuated with the nomadic tents of isolated farmers.And then my first sighting of a yak,an animal that I will come to depend upon for sustenance in the days ahead. This is surely an I-Spy book cliché: how many points for both a yak and yurt?

Thinking through my memories of the night spent tossing and turning in my berth, I recall someone joining us at one point. My memory comes back to the surface when I next peer in through the gap in the door of our compartment. My cabin mates are both sitting up in their beds, dressed in their puffa jackets and breathing from oxygen nose-tubes. They look far worse than I feel. I think they must have called for help in the night, but I must have been comatose or delirious at the time. I don't remember anyone offering me any oxygen. I smile at them and make a thumbs-up sign. Andy does his best to look happy, but they are clearly both miserable. They decline my offer of tea, but that's understandable; what self-respecting Chinese person would trust a westerner to make their tea?

The train crosses the Tanggula Pass at 07.00, and here we arrive at a solitary platform in the middle of absolutely nowhere. This is a place of significance to anyone with an interest in railway history; at 5068 metres, it's the highest railway station in the world. The record had previously been held by the Peruvian railway station at Ticlio, but the prize moved here in in 2006 with the arrival of the first Lhasa-bound passenger train. There isn't much to see here, and that shouldn't be a surprise as Tanggula is uninhabited. But nonetheless on the platform stands a small building and a timetable poster. The only sign I can see just says 'Tang Gu La' in English and Chinese ('la' is Tibetan for 'pass'), together with the altitude. I'm surprised the Chinese rail marketing men haven't built something with more bells and whistles to recognise its record-breaking status. Our scheduled two-minute stop completed, no passengers get off or on and we set off, dipping down the valley. We are going to descend to Lhasa at a comparatively comfortable 3650 metres.

When we reach Nagchu at around 8.30 am, I decide to stretch my legs and try to breathe some fresh unenriched air. The guard who does most of the paperwork and ticketing agrees with me that this is going to be a 20-minute stop, denoted in international sign language by two fingers and a pointing gesture at one's watch. The only problem is that it's just a six-minute stop. I'm just a couple of carriages away when I realise something's wrong and dive for the nearest set of doors. The guard doesn't recognise me, and my gold card is in my compartment. I have left all my paperwork and even my jacket on the train, so I have to dash back to my own carriage, and I get there just in time. But it gets me thinking what I would have done if the doors had closed and the train started leaving without me. Two choices: jump onto one of the carriage steps and hang on in the hope that someone spots you, or give up and find a vehicle to catch up with the train. Hanging on was what Gene Wilder did in the classic 1976 train film 'Silver Streak'. I even achieved this feat myself in Germany a couple of years ago. But hanging onto the outside of this train, below freezing and in the thin air, I don't think I would last five minutes. I would have to find a yak herder with a motorbike and travel cross country. Mindful of these possibilities, I'm thankful to be back on board the Z21, even if it does smell badly of cigarette smoke and stink fruit.

By mid-morning Andy and Rachel are off the oxygen and eating again. They snack continually, and I'm fed a stream of apparently altitude-beating Chinese medicine. They look on approvingly as I consume it. Then a man I haven't seen before steps in. He's some sort of medical official, possibly even a doctor. He asks Andy a few questions, and looks very serious about the subject being discussed. With a few notes made in his little notebook, he leaves us. I seem to have been invisible to the healthcare provided on this train. The assumption is that I'm fine, which is okay because I think I'm fine too. Despite the nausea of altitude, the rest of the passengers in our carriage continue to eat stunning quantities of instant noodles. But I have no appetite at all – I have had just one proper meal in the last three days. So I've started adding sugar to my tea for energy, and I'm drinking what feels a lot in an effort to be fully hydrated, which can be a big factor in acclimatisation.

The sun shining through the compartment window is strong and comforting even with the special glass to reduce the radiation from its rays. I would describe my mood as high on life, but actually I think I'm high on the lack of oxygen. The colours of the landscape are saturated and I feel light-headed, even woozy. We stop every now and again and wait for a train to pass in the other direction, as there is only a single line on difficult sections of the track. Eventually mountain passes become river valleys, and small settlements begin to appear next to the line. Then toward lunchtime the huts become small concrete buildings, and as we round the river plain, multi-storey buildings, cars and concrete roads signal our arrival into the outskirts of Lhasa.

Chapter Thirteen:
Seven Days in Tibet

Tenzing is standing in front of a black SUV about 100 metres in front of the station. Dressed in a down jacket and military-style shades, and with short hair and well-tanned skin he could easily pass for a mountaineer, but his main occupation is as an official government guide. Without his services my permit to travel here would not have been issued. He has probably spotted me well before I guess who he is. I suspect he might have a dossier in the car with a mugshot of me and some notes on my habits. As my eyes adjust to the intensity of the sunshine outside the ticket hall I have my first glimpse of Tibetan architecture; not an ancient temple, but a modern railway station interpreted in the style of an ancient Tibetan temple. Whitewashed angular uprights and windows supported by brown stonework. But the strangest thing is not the building itself but the space around it; with bollards and barriers prevent anyone from driving near the place it's dead concrete ground with no purpose other than separation. The station is a massive statement of achievement, yet incongruous in this environment, as though it belongs to a different world and has to be protected.

Tenzing greets me with a warm handshake and a smile that I will come to know and love in the days ahead. With him is Pasang, the driver of our shiny Chinese executive vehicle. With my bags loaded, we set off down the quiet and well-ordered streets in the direction of my hotel. I wish I could just relax, but I'm still in solo not-trusting-anyone mode. I fire a few questions at Tenzing, which he answers carefully with occasional pauses for thought. His English is near-perfect. Once I have established that Tenzing knows my plans and has my paperwork, I sit back and listen to him laugh and joke with Pasang. My first impression is that they both seem incredibly happy in themselves.

Not having eaten anything fresh for a few days, I feel the time is right to try some food. I'm sure there is an approved list of culturally suitable places to take a foreigner to eat, but I'm surprised by the choice of venue. Pasang pulls up outside a low-rise block covered in advertising boards in a busy suburban market square. Tenzing shows me up some rickety wooden stairs and into a Tibetan pizzeria. To be fair, it does sell things other than pizza, but this is clearly its speciality. The manageress looks pleased to see us, and ushers us to a dusty table near the fire. The menu in English lists all sorts of pizzas, most based around yak meat and cheese. I have found that when engaging the services of a guide, it's quite normal for the guide to leave you and to eat separately, so I'm delighted when not only does Tenzing sit down and peruse the menu, but Pasang as well. Yak pizza all round, washed down with warm Coke. Hardly a gourmet introduction to Tibetan cuisine, but I must have had a cheese craving as it tasted divine. It must be the altitude. I expect my Coca-Cola has been bottled a long way away. The railway has undoubtedly increased the range of food available on the plateau, as well as introducing some global brands.

At the hotel reception desk, a lady with a lovely smile takes my passport, and types about me at length on her keyboard. Tenzing insists I try to speak to her in Tibetan, my first indication of how much local people want to protect and preserve their culture and identity. 'Tashi delak, he tutors me, means Hello. Then you say Kayrang kusu debo-yimbay? It means How are you?' I do my best and after the receptionist has stopped laughing, she produces a room key and some paperwork. Saying goodbye to Tenzing I head to the lift. We will meet again tomorrow morning when I have rested and will have acclimatised a bit more.

The next hour or two is spent washing off the grime of long-distance rail travel and reorganising my belongings. Travel in this age involves a lot of things that need recharging, and I carry a bag of connectors, adapters, cables, and even more spare cables. It takes up valuable space in my bag, but I have learned that if you carry a spare cable then the main cable never fails. It's the law of Sod. Assembling a line of devices, I get the first couple plugged in. But something isn't right – my iPad isn't charging. Checking the connections, I pull out the connector and reinsert it. A blue flash and an electric shock shoots through my hand and I drop it onto the bed. My tablet is now blank, devoid of life. I have become far too reliant on this one device and having no iPad would be a disaster. I spend the next 20 minutes in a state of moderate panic trying to restore it to life. At last it fires up, but the mains port won't work, so when the battery runs out that'll be it. But at least I can now connect it to the internet and look for solutions. A search reveals that in very dry environments it is possible for the current to arc from the cable to the port via your body, and this is what must have happened. With great relief I perform a series of recovery steps and it starts to accept a charge, but it won't allow me to plug in my memory card adapter. There is nothing I can do about this until I reach a city with an Apple store. Probably Hong Kong.

I'm too tired to trust myself to take just a nap on the very comfy-looking bed, so instead I take a wander around the hotel. It's a big building and the place is deserted. I wonder where everyone is hiding. In the basement I walk past a door with a sign on it saying 'Oxygen Room'. I have spotted oxygen bottles complete with masks outside some of the bedrooms; you can order them on room service. But down here in the bowels of the building is a sealed room containing enriched air, where people with symptoms of altitude sickness can recover. It's an impressive facility, but I decide to give it a miss. I'm not feeling too bad, and I wonder if this might actually slow down the acclimatisation process. Down the corridor is a small health club, also as busy as the Marie Celeste. I retrace my steps to Reception and convince them to send someone to fire up the steam room. This is uncharted territory for me. Is a steam room a good thing or a bad thing at high altitude? Does steam have more oxygen, less oxygen or the same amount of oxygen than normal air at a given altitude? Answers on a postcard please.

It isn't until breakfast the next day that I meet any other guests at the hotel. A mix of Chinese businessmen and western tourists, mainly French. Behind a

polished steel counter, Chef cooks eggs to order –
the eggs of what bird I'm not entirely sure, but they
taste good. Reasonable coffee helps me shake off the
fatigue of broken sleep and weird dreams, another
side-effect of the altitude. Tenzing and Pasang are
waiting for me in Reception. As they greet me I feel
that they're assessing how well I have survived the
night and if I'm up to today's plans. Tibetan greetings,
smiles all round, and we head off north of the city to
visit the Sera Monastery.

Founded in 1419, Sera is a large area with dozens
of colleges and hermitages where the monks and
nuns go about their business. We have to abandon
the vehicle, so Pasang stays behind to mind it. He
doesn't like to leave it out of his sight. Climbing
a rocky path, I find the slight incline challenging, and I wheeze and splutter my way upward.
Tenzing provides frequent words of encourage-
ment, at first welcomed, but before long just adding
to my frustration, as they expose my inability to
climb at the speed of passing 96-year-old nuns. We
pass brass bells and prayer wheels attached to the
mountainside. Joining in the ritual, I spin the wheels
and knock the bells to send prayers.

Inside the entrance of the monastery, steep
cobbled paths lead off in several directions.
There isn't a cloud in the deep blue sky, and the
sunlight bounces off the whitewashed walls.

They're dazzling without sunglasses, and I can understand why most of the monks have such impressive sun tans. Their deep red robes stand out against the buildings and are hugely photogenic. Climbing the big steps up to the Great Assembly Hall we come across a huge shiny metal dish. My first guess is that it's to receive satellite television, but looking more closely I see it has no electronic connections, just a big kettle in front of it. Ingenious. The monks make their tea using solar power. The polished dish reflects the sun in a tight beam at a specific spot in front of it. Wondering how long it takes to boil the kettle, I remember some schoolboy physics: water boils at 100°C at sea level, but the boiling point is reduced by 1°C for every 300-metre gain in height. My oxygen-starved brain can't do the maths, but I reckon that up here we're talking about the possibility of a reasonable cup of chai at around 80°C.

Inside the hall, I follow the pilgrims around the statues and scriptures that line the walls of the building. Many pilgrims have travelled across Tibet to visit Sera: some from other parts of China, and even India. The ritual at each of the shrines and holy relics is to push tiny denomination banknotes into donation boxes to guarantee good luck in a future life. Special monks manage the money and take the full boxes of cash to an even bigger box in another part of the room. Thus the pilgrims feel they are gaining spiritual benefit through their donations, and the monks are receiving a valuable source of income to feed and clothe the residents of the monastery. The business of giving also involves money changers who split small-denomination yuan notes into even smaller denomination jiao ones. I have never seen a jiao before: it's worth a tenth of a yuan, less than one British penny.

Sera is famous for its public afternoon debates when monks challenge each other to defend and answer questions – but today for an undisclosed reason there is to be no debate. Around the corner from where the monks usually ask and answer questions, we come across the long line of crying children, the place where Tenzing and I got locked in the little-used outbuilding containing the mandala. I'm pleased to tell you that we eventually escape through the door we went in by. There's no giant rolling boulder, no pit of snakes to jump over. Just a monk, amused by the text from Tenzing on his mobile.

After our ordeal, we find a small restaurant and, whilst telling Pasang what happened, we drink tea. Not any old tea, but Tibetan butter tea, an interesting concoction of yak butter, salt and tea leaves served in little steaming bowls. Tenzing explains that the butter provides cheap sustenance and even protects the lips from the dry atmosphere. It tastes pretty rough to me, but I don't want to miss out on a tradition that goes back to the Tang dynasty of the 7th to 10th centuries. Revitalised by the tea, I stroll the streets and squares of the city in the afternoon, alone. Of course, it's possible that Tenzing is keeping an eye on me from a distance. If he is, he must be deep undercover as I can't spot him. The shops are all piled high with rugs, musical instruments and Tibetan temple memorabilia. In the street, waves of pilgrims, tourists and beggars cross in different directions. Then I spot men high on the rooftops looking down on the crowd through big pairs of binoculars. What are they looking for?

The next day, Tenzing takes me to visit the summer palace. It's a pleasant stroll through the gardens between the brightly coloured buildings and pavilions. But there is something here that I find both intriguing and hard to understand; amidst the gardens stands a building that was once the home of the 14th Dalai Lama until his sudden departure in 1956. In Tibet in general, there is much sensitivity around him, in both native Tibetans and in a different way by the Chinese administration; I'm not even permitted to carry a book around containing an image of his holiness. But strangely, here at his former home in the summer palace, there are not just pictures of his life, but also artefacts: his bed, his desk, even an early television set. I had been

175

expecting Tenzing to not want to talk much about this, but he turns out to be something of a cultural contradiction. As well as being a thoroughly decent and well-educated person, he is both an official Chinese government guide and a proud Tibetan. He seems relaxed about my cultural concerns, and chats openly about most topics of conversation. Standing in the sunshine looking back at the building, I ask him something about the events that took place here in 1956. He pauses, but before he can say anything a suited official standing nearby says something to him in Chinese. My thoughts are firstly why such a person would understand English and be listening in, and secondly what he might now be saying to Tenzing. I don't ask for an explanation of this, but draw my own conclusion. Things are perhaps not all as they might at first seem. After that incident, and while we walk back towards the car, I remain silent. My questions can wait until later.

That evening in the steam room I reflect on my experiences so far of life in Tibet. The more I see the more I am confused by what is in my opinion good and what is not so good. All that I can be really sure of at this stage is how charming the Tibetan people are. Every single one I have met has been cheerful and welcoming.

After I leave the steam room what next? Nightlife isn't a big thing in Lhasa, and the most exciting thing going on in my part of town is the hotel disco. In a room full of neon lights a three-piece band warm up, and I'm not keen on what I hear. It's a cacophony of feedback and Asian hard rock with some ethnic vocals thrown over the top. So I relocate to the bar, where I'm served a warm bottle of lager. In response to me asking why they are warm, even from inside the fridge, a lady explains that that is how people like beer here; it's so cold outside at night that they prefer to drink their beer warm. I think I have just found the first thing that I'm not keen on in Tibetan life.

A trip to the Jokang Temple the next afternoon proves to be an eye-opening experience. Past the shopping streets of downtown Lhasa sits one of the most holy places in Tibet, and I'm greeted by the sight of hundreds of pilgrims outside. They don't stand or walk towards the temple, though. They crawl. They arch their bodies forwards and backwards praying towards the shrine outside the temple building. Stepping around and at times over them I follow Tenzing inside. Tenzing is Mr Lhasa; he seems to know everyone, and everyone knows him. He greets everyone with a warm smile and a handshake, and from the way he speaks to people and listens so carefully to their answers, I think he has built up a lot of respect in these parts. Here we seem to be magicked from the back of a long queue straight into the main building. Up some stairs and

we're on the gilded roof of the temple, looking out over the people below. In the distance
are big mountains, perhaps the foothills of the
Himalayas and in the opposite direction are
low-rise flat-roofed shops with wide pedestrianised
streets. I spot more men on the roof opposite,
sheltering from the sun under a little gazebo. One
stares through his binoculars whilst the other is using
a walkie-talkie. I point them out to Tenzing, who
immediately tells me not to point at them.

Sprawled out on the bed in my cosy hotel room
that evening, I watch 'The Man Who Would be
King' again. It's impossible to watch this film too
many times. It's an epic British film based on the
Kipling tale about two soldiers who travel from
India into Central Asia where they discover a
remote kingdom ruled by a strange religion. But
tonight it doesn't take my breath away like it
normally does, and I think this is because the mountains and the temples no longer look at all unusual to
me. It's as though I've been wandering about the film
set every day I've been here in Lhasa – parts of the
monasteries and palaces here date back to before
the 7th century and feel completely untouched by
the progress of time.

The following morning is a big one. Tenzing has
organised a visit to the Potala Palace, the winter
residence of the Dalai Lama since 1694, and built

on the site of a much older palace. Entrance is by ticket only, and only 700 are available for each day. The palace is so important to the pilgrims that tickets are often sold out well in advance. To get inside we will join them in the steep climb to the top of the palace. Pasang finds a parking spot as we hop out into the frozen early morning air; the sun has yet to creep over the top of the Red Hill that the palace was built on. It towers overhead more than 300 metres above our heads. On top of this are 13 storeys of palace, housing more than 1000 rooms. Tenzing tells me there are more than 10,000 shrines to visit here today. That's going to be a lot more than all the shrines I have seen in my entire life. I hope that I don't become 'templed out'.

The timing of our visit has been deliberate, so that before attempting the climb I will have had as long as possible in Lhasa to acclimatise; this is sadly going to be my last full day in Lhasa. It's not that big a climb, but at over 1000 steps it still presents something of a challenge for pressure-balanced lifeforms like me who are used to living at sea level. My initial pace is too fast, and I have to stop after just a couple of minutes' walking. Tenzing has seen this all before. He encourages me to stop as often as I like, and stays with me as we climb from the cobbled path onto flights of stone steps, zig-zagging up the dark side of the palace. Each and every tall step is an effort and I set myself the target of just reaching the next turn where I can stop and let my breathing catch up whilst I take in the view back down. When we reach the ticket office Tenzing completes the red tape whilst I say a quick hello to a small group of Americans. They are climbers, and although I don't have time to find out their plan, I imagine it is likely to be Mount Everest. I'm sure they are in the right place for a blessing.

When we stop every five minutes or so to allow me to recover from my breathless state, and whilst I wheeze and bend double, Tenzing chats to the locals. Is there anyone he doesn't know? Some of the pilgrims have the same problem as me, whilst those who have travelled here from the mountains just skip past us. Finally, after about an hour we reach the top floor of the edifice and step inside, through some little wooden doors. At first we go into an outer courtyard, then up some rickety wooden stairs and along a passageway into the palace itself.

It takes a while for my eyes to adjust to the dark wooden interior, but once they have I sense that I have travelled back in time again. The year could be 1694, 1994 or the present day. Absolutely nothing has changed. Through a smokescreen of incense, all I can see at first are crowds of people shuffling forwards. The pilgrims are mesmerised by the shrines; they move from one to the next in an unorganised procession overseen by the monks. Holy men chant, offer prayers and generally supervise the process of receiving the offerings of vast amounts of small-denomination bank notes. As I get close to the first shrine I can't quite believe what is in front of me. The deities are not just dripping in gold, but covered in precious stones. There are no glass panels, vaults or alarms here. Pilgrims reach out and touch their incalculable worth.

Tenzing knows the place like the back of his hand, which is just as well as without him I would be hopelessly lost in moments. Several times I see him stopping pilgrims and pointing them in a different direction. He leads me up a wooden staircase and into a large chamber with even larger shrines; the statues here have been made from solid gold. As we leave one of the galleries, a nun approaches Tenzing. He has an amazingly polite and respectful way with anyone he meets; he nods his head and smiles at the end of every sentence. There is a lot of nodding and smiling going on in this conversation. He tells me that the nun has noticed that I wear glasses, and would I like my vision restored? I think about this for a moment, and wonder if there is a downside to the procedure. Tenzing doesn't say it, but his look and body language suggest to me that this is not a service one declines. Following the nun around a corner and down a dark corridor we reach a mandala, this one a painting, hanging on the wall. I put some money in the box, and wait. A monk stares at the painting, transfixed by its intricate geometric patterns. He is creating a sacred space using the guidance of the mandala, and once he is in its focus he performs a blessing upon me. I will let you know what my optician says about my eyesight when I next have a check-up.

The significance of each individual shrine is explained to me at first, but after a while I wonder if even the keenest pilgrim can absorb the story of every one of them. I shuffle past some shrines respectfully, but also thinking that some fresh air would be good soon, as I've smoked the equivalent of five packs of joss sticks in here. I'm presented with a white prayer scarf by a monk on one of the lower levels, and told that I can place it on the altar and make a wish. When I do this a gong is gently banged, my wish accepted. Rather than wishing for world peace, more pragmatically I have asked for a more peaceful onward rail journey to my next destination, Guangzhou, more than 5000 kilometres away.

Chapter Fourteen:
Slow Train to Canton

Life in Lhasa has been good, and other than the altitude, easy going. With Tenzing at my side, getting by has been easy and worry-free. Even without him, the warmth of every Tibetan I met makes me think life would be good here if I were on my own. But all good things come to an end, and today I have to say goodbye to my amazing companions. I'm going to become a solo traveller again, and with that the responsibility for looking after myself; I like travelling alone, but it requires a different mindset to remain content. Everyone has their own way of dealing with this, some more successfully than others; for me the vital step change is to stop worrying about unimportant things and live in the moment. The challenge of course is to decide what's important enough to worry about, and what is superfluous. Perspective is all-important.

On the way to the railway station we stop at a supermarket. I'm a bit surprised to find a supermarket here, but I realise that it's probably down to the railway supply chain that modern groceries and household brands are available in Lhasa. Here I find all that I need for my trip: noodles, beer, fresh fruit and soft toilet roll. The supermarket almost certainly sells yak meat too, but I have no plans to make any pizza or stew on the train. On reflection I haven't been shown any open food markets here, which is strange, as it's normally one of the first places you get taken to as a traveller in any new city in Asia. Perhaps this was intentional, to demonstrate what a modern and prosperous city Lhasa has become. Any yak meat on sale here has been carefully butchered by someone wearing a white coat, and sealed in plastic packaging – none of the horrors of the usual Asian meat markets, where live creatures are held captive in baskets and cut up to order on bloodstained wooden chopping blocks. A smartly dressed cashier rings up my items, looking approvingly at my choice of instant noodles. They must be the connoisseurs' choice. She points to the amount next to her computerised till. 'Cledit card?' she asks.

At the railway station, I wish Pasang all the best, then Tenzing escorts me as far as the security checkpoint and we say our goodbyes. Shaking his hand and giving him a hug, I surprise myself once more with how emotional I become. It must be the altitude. I hope I get to meet him again someday. He looks on as I load my bags onto the x-ray belt (without falling onto it this time) and then I pass through the security scanner. A small huddle of uniformed officials stare at the monitor looking for prohibited items. I have no idea what my bag might look like on the screen; the combination of miles of cables, spare batteries, tools, and supplies must look pretty weird. The man sitting in the middle of the group points at the image of my bag and speaks to a guard opposite. 'Knife,' he says to me. 'You have knife?' I do indeed. Several in fact. Opening my big bag, I fish out my trusty Swiss Army knife first. It's the Climber model, the one with a pair of scissors in addition to the usual range of blades and implements for fixing horse hooves and disgorging hooks from the mouths of large fish. The guard picks up my knife and examines it with some suspicion before depositing it in a nearby plastic laundry basket. 'No knife,' he says and hands me a piece of paper which turns out to be a receipt. Tenzing translates as I try to explain to him that this knife has travelled on trains across China several times, but he is having none of it. It isn't allowed here, apparently, and this isn't the same as in the rest of China. Had I time to think about it I would have shown him my eating knife first instead. I bet he would have just taken that. But now I'm without an object not only of huge practical value, but something I regard, like my thermos flask, as rather lucky. It's been through so much with me that I don't like to be without it. But there is nothing I can do so, being practical, I give my receipt to Tenzing so he can reclaim it. A final handshake over the barriers, and I'm on my own again.

Like the rest of China, the station has waiting rooms, and after my tickets and permit have been checked yet again, I'm directed up a flight of stairs to the one for my train. Inside it is already full and the noise level is incredible. Do I detect a slight pause in the hubbub as I walk in, or is it just my imagination? Once again, I'm the only farang here and the locals find me fascinating. Finding a vacant plastic chair behind a pile of bags in the corner, I try to blend in as best as I can. The passengers in the room are mostly in small groups, and their faces are brown and wrinkled with hard work in the sun; pilgrims, farmers perhaps, and families travelling from remote parts of the plateau.

It only takes half a second of an announcement on the public address system to cause a mass scramble to the gate. Queuing isn't a well practised custom in these parts, but barging and bundling is an Olympic sport. Once through another ticket check, I follow the herd down onto the platform where the now familiar-looking carriages await us. This one is the Z266, a service which now runs daily from Lhasa to Guangzhou (Canton), nearly 4400 kilometres away. I can't remember why I chose to book this leg as a single journey, but I must have been in an odd frame of mind at the time to have done so. This is a big trip, but I'm treating it like a short journey. I suspect I'm the only person travelling all the way to Canton. How many Chinese people would want to do this? To a European it would be like wanting to take a single train journey from Edinburgh to Istanbul without getting off at Paris, Munich or Venice.

Down on the platform I quickly manage to locate carriage number 6, my home for the next three days. I'm in a lower berth this time, which is good, but the compartment is already full of occupants and their bags, which is not so good. Fortunately they are friendly, and rearrange everything to fit my luggage in without any fuss. Looking round, my first impressions are that it's pretty comfy in here. We even have plastic flowers and net curtains. Chinese rolling stock is often more modern than you might think it's going to be from the outside. Carriages on slow trains often look older than they are because of the way that the outside is painted a dull matt green. It's almost a military look. If I were the marketing manager for Chinese Railways I would immediately rebrand, and paint them all in some sort of brighter and jazzier style. The layout of the carriage is similar to the one

I arrived in, apart from there now being just a single, rather grim, squat toilet at one end. Z trains are not actually that slow; this train only makes 11 stops in its 4400-kilometre run back up over Tanggula, and then through central China before it turns south-wards towards Guangzhou. Tomorrow it will stop at Lanzhou at lunchtime (12.49), then not again until it gets into Zhengzhou, the capital of Henan Province, the next morning at 03.13; that's over 14 hours and 1200 kilometres between stops.

A guard squeezes into our compartment and hands out the by now familiar plastic gold cards in exchange for our tickets. The system is actually quite a good one, as they swap them back when you will be getting off at the next stop. Because they have your ticket, they know you are on the train, and when you get your ticket back you know it's time to get off. As well as the gold card, I'm handed a little form. It's in Chinese, so I have no idea what it's for. Pointing at it, the guard realises this and exchanges it for one with a rather strange English translation. It's a health declaration that would seem to make it clear I'm travelling up here very much at my own risk. This is slightly bizarre, as I had no form to complete on the journey up here. Noting a variety of conditions that would preclude travel, I tick some boxes, sign it and hand it back to him.

The chaps in my carriage look to be experienced rail travellers. They fall into their own space and text their loved ones. I don't manage to find out their names, but I understand they are on business and travelling to Xian, the first major city once we've got back onto the main line. But first we have to cross back over the Tanggula and down to Golmud. If all goes to plan the train's altitude will be significantly lower at bedtime, and some sleep might be on the cards tonight. The queuing and barging has clearly tired me out, as I slump back on my berth and watch the world pass by, both inside and out. The door to our compartment is open, and whenever I look up there are a couple of Tibetans or ethnic Chinese standing there staring at me as though I am an alien from outer space. This gets quite tiresome, but I'm not closing the door, as I like the open 'drop-in' feel of the carriage. The kids also like to shout 'Hello!' at me and then disappear before I can further test their English language skills.

As the train climbs back up to the highest railway station in the world at Tanggula, I feel more acclimatised than I did on the way up from Beijing, but it's still hard work just doing nothing. Idling allows me to dwell on my physical state and my environment in a rather negative way. As my sinuses are bunged up, I have earache from a pressure squeeze in my them that I can't seem to clear. I have cracked lips and a split tongue from trying to get enough of the thin dry air into my lungs. I have a headache, and I also have a mild dose of Khumbu cough, the one that climbers get that can break ribs. I have a stomach ache and I haven't eaten much at all in over two days. But perhaps worst of all I'm beginning to feel sick and wretched because the locals are smoking at each end of the corridor.

Our stop at Tanggula is once again brief, and I can't see anyone actually getting onto or off the train. The phrase 'it's all downhill from here' comes to my mind. In just a few hours I hope to be slurping great lungfuls of rich humidified air. There seems to be little or no oxygen being pumped into the compartment. The profile of our climb up from Lhasa isn't as extreme as the journey on the other side from Beijing. It's only a guess, but perhaps coming from Lhasa we are deemed as already acclimatised, and the oxygen is reserved for inbound passengers. It takes real effort to rummage around in my bags and find some pills for my headache. Hot sweet tea keeps me conscious as we descend, and later in the afternoon, as we leave the raised section of the line that keeps the tracks above the permafrost, I can feel the train speed up. We must be approaching the edge of the Tibetan Plateau, and I decide now is the time to switch from speaking Tibetan back to Chinese. It's not a big deal, though, as I speak perhaps a dozen words of badly pronounced Chinese and only four of Tibetan. Kha-ley-phe (farewell), Tibet!

Sleep is once again elusive, and although we are definitely lower now I cough and splutter through most of the night. I'm sensitive to smoke, and can smell someone lighting up anywhere in our carriage. Eventually around dawn, I fall into the sort of sleep you only get when your body is totally exhausted. But I can't have been unconscious for long when I feel a gentle but firm tug on my ankle. Lifting my eyeshade, I see the guard is standing over me, looking down. Sitting up, I'm dazed and confused. She returns my ticket in exchange for the gold card. Then she surprises me by getting out her smartphone and pointing to the translated words 'change train' and 'one hour'. This wasn't my plan – I'd understood that this train was going to Guangzhou, my next destination. At least she has given me an hour to prepare. I check my diary for the day; the page is blank, so I add 'Z266, change trains at Xining'. Time to pack.

I'm ready to go for this unexplained excursion as we glide into West Xining. The lines are incredibly smooth. There are railway staff already in position on the platform, awaiting our arrival. It is immediately clear that this is a normal procedure, and the train has been matched to an identical-looking one on the platform opposite.

The new carriage number 6 is about 10 metres away from the old one. I have never before experienced such a simple connection. You have to be a bit of a train anorak to spot the differences between the trains. In the new carriage the fake flowers are a bit less sophisticated, and there is about six inches less floor space, possibly because the berths are wider. I can only assume the un-timetabled switch is so that they can keep the special high-altitude carriages for the upper stretch of the line. We didn't have to make this change on the inbound Beijing train, but this is a less prestigious service. With the luggage re-stowed, I make up a fresh bed and crash out until lunchtime. My companions make noodles and continue to send thousands of text messages.

Waking up on an unfamiliar train can be disorientating until you remember where you are. There are few immediate clues, and most train compartments look pretty similar. But today it's easy; the smell of cheap cigarettes and the sound of excitably spoken Mandarin in the corridor, and I know exactly where I am. I decide to break the cycle of my negative thought by taking a short walk to the restaurant carriage. The new dining carriage is quieter and a little less smoky than the old one, so I nurse a glass of hot water and tea leaves and read a book there until I get told to leave. Staff don't like lingerers, I think, mainly as they are government employees working set hours with formal breaks, so off-shift the restaurant becomes their staff canteen. I reluctantly put my book back into my bag and head back to the madhouse that is also known as carriage number 6. Opening the outer door, I find that the smell of stale food, body odour and cigarette smoke has reached a newly repressive level. I'm on the brink of losing my perspective on this. But whilst I fret about the conditions in the carriage, I barely notice that outside the landscape is changing. The tracks are now passing through low-lying valleys and river plains. There don't seem to be many people living here; just occasional tented farms with herds of animals, mostly yak. The sun gradually moves down to the skyline of the hills and darkness creeps over the scenery. I have a sense of foreboding about night-time on this train.

My bowels have been locked solid since I left Lhasa, and I realise I'm going to have to face the hostile environment of the toilet before bed, or risk having to get up in the night. I find it strange that the brain can interrupt the digestive process based on the lack of acceptable facilities, but it can only delay the inevitable for so long. My choices are limited on this train. There should be two toilets in each carriage, one squatter and one western, but on this train the western ones are locked. I don't know if this is a staff perk, or just to minimise cleaning, but it means that there are 32 passengers per toilet. You might think this is a strange statistic to consider, but it's a good indicator of the likely sanitation. By comparison in SV class on the Vostok, the ratio was just 8 passengers per toilet.

Passing the open-plan washing area, I jump over a couple of puddles of indeterminate liquid. At the sinks, people prepare their dinners, wash their clothes and brush their teeth, some all at the same time. Opposite is the toilet door, and all that stands between it and me is an old man in a black leather coat and matching hat. He stares at me, spits on the floor and smiles with a gap-toothed grin. He's not waiting to use the toilet though, just standing next to it. I could think of lots of places to stand and stare at people, but this would not be on my list. He steps to one side and ushers me in. But stepping inside reveals that this is not a toilet, but a gas chamber. This toilet has been repurposed as a smoking room, and I have to retreat immediately wheezing and feeling nauseous. The man outside smiles at me again and offers me a cigarette.

The toilet in the next carriage is almost as bad, but I don't have much time to be fussy. The floor is covered in faeces and detritus, and concentration is required to find a safe way to reach the little hole in the floor. A perverse game of Twister. On a journey of this length any accident would be serious, so I take my time taking off clothing that might become contaminated and finding something clean to hang on to. Strange to consider that I'm in the country with the largest and longest high-speed network in the world. But that is a world far away from the Z train to Canton.

My mission almost complete, I feel a sense of mild euphoria. After all, what could be any worse than this? Everything has to be better now. In the manner of someone cleaning themselves up after potential exposure to an Ebola outbreak, I open my bag of soap and wet wipes. Turning on the hot water tap, of course nothing comes out of the stained orifice. The cold-water tap however, oozes a drizzle of rust-coloured water into the tarnished steel basin, which has no plug. I scrub my hands and limbs until they hurt, and with my bag repacked, retrace my steps to the door. When I get off the train I shall throw my flip-flops away.

Back in the compartment there is an eerie glow of smartphones in the darkness. It's an oppressive environment with the heat, smoke and noise. I arrange my night kit on the table, or at least the 50% of it that I claim as my own as a lower-berth passenger. Eyeshades, earplugs, torch, clock and water. All I'm missing is my trusty Swiss Army knife. Lying on top of the bedding in my clothes I try and zone out, and I imagine myself onto a beach somewhere in South East Asia. I get as far as imagining a cool breeze and a cold beer in my hand, when the man above fancies a cigarette and steps on my ankle as he climbs down from the upper berth.

From time to time I get up and go for a walk. It's cooler in the corridor, and now that most of the crazy passengers are in bed there's less smoking going on. In the night I meet some interesting characters. A man wearing a jacket with an enormous snorkel hood has decided to sleep outside on the floor. Maybe he has fallen out with the passengers in his compartment? I carefully step over him as I wander down to the end of the carriage where the once-busy wash area is now quiet. A student is charging a huge laptop computer from the shaver socket. He speaks some English, and it's nice to be able to talk to someone. He has that geeky but commercially hungry look about him that tells me one day he will be a billionaire, and probably quite soon. With no one else to talk to I get back into my berth and fall into a fitful sleep.

Something feels different the next morning. Lifting my eye shades, I see bright light streaming round the edges of the window blind. My puffy eyes adjust to the gloom. I'm alone. I must have slept through the departure of my cabin mates in the night. Their bedding has gone, too, and as it has not been replaced, I'm thinking I might have the place to myself today. It's an effort, but I decide to clean the compartment and reorganise it for solo occupation. It's easy to be uncomfortable, but much better to make things as good as they can be. I now have four pillows to myself, so I fashion a chaise longue with the spare bedding. Raising the blind, I'm greeted by rain and mist. I have no clue as to where we are. I see blocks of flats bigger than any I have seen so far, and they have individual air conditioning units, so I sense we are on the edge of domestic prosperity. It's also a signal that we must now be a lot further south, where the climate would justify owning such a device, assuming you could afford one.

Although I have no appetite for food, I spend a lot of time thinking about it; I've been on the rails long enough to have cravings for all sorts of things. Normally after a few weeks in Asia, I fantasise about toasted cheese sandwiches, but my thoughts right now are totally focused on a roast dinner. I can't decide if it's beef or chicken, but either way it would include Yorkshire pudding and all the trimmings. I have to face up to the fact, though, that whilst almost any big hotel can make a passable toasted cheese sandwich, my chances of getting a roast dinner in the days ahead are slim. Lateral thinking is required. I need to find the Chinese equivalent of a roast dinner. Maybe it's duck with a special sauce. But I can't make this work in my head unless it comes with a honey roast parsnips and thick gravy.

There is little to do here on my own. Once I have cleaned the place up and rearranged the plastic flowers, I'm bored. I can't decide what to read. To keep myself entertained I binge watch some classic television episodes: 'Fawlty Towers' always makes me laugh and puts me in a good mood. The train is much quieter now as we speed through flatter terrain towards Guangzhou. I get the impression that most passengers have alighted in central China; I infer that between the big cities of the south people can afford tickets on high-speed trains, and it would not make sense to spend the day on a slow train unless you were going to sleep on it. So, with no passengers to organise, the guards have disappeared. My guess is that they are drinking tea in the restaurant carriage. Later in the day I do spot one with a mop and bucket, which is a bit of a surprise to both of us. Without the smoke, the shouting and the spitting, I'm beginning to feel quite settled. If only the whole journey could have been like this.

According to my timetable our altitude in Guang-dong province is now just 28 metres above sea level and I'm enjoying the rich air. This train ride has certainly – and unexpectedly – been one of the most challenging ones of this trip and I will be pleased to get off tonight. But every adventure has both good bits and not-so-good bits. Putting things into perspective, I haven't been robbed, chased by wild bears or detained in a cell. This is just life as a rail adventurer. If everything went smoothly, there would be much less enjoyment of the good things, and no rose-tinted nostalgia of the misery.

Chapter Fifteen:
Way of the Dragon

My first visit to Canton was in 1990. Mainland China seemed very adventurous to me back then; with a simple tourist visa issued, I embarked on a short escorted tour from Hong Kong. Canton was a big city then, but nothing like the size it is today. The city now has several railway stations, and I realise that my hotel is a long way from where I have arrived. My taxi driver becomes increasingly sinister as our journey unfolds. He's on the phone to his friends, and he's telling them about me. At one point he says something really creepy, like 'You're mine now.' I can only hope I'm not locked in a car with Guangzhou's answer to Doctor Hannibal Lecter. I try and avoid conversation, and wonder if the highway we are on is in fact taking me in the right direction. I'm worried enough to decide to turn on the data on my phone to follow where we are headed. It turns out that he's just joking, though, and safely across the city he deposits me at a modern hotel close to Guangzhou East station, where I can catch a train to Hong Kong.

One of the weirder aspects of rail adventure is the switching between living on and living off the rails. There is a period of decompression where you normalise the new state of either moving or not moving, and the new norms of your surroundings. The concierge must have sensed my disorientation, as he escorts me up to my room and makes sure I'm okay. It's late in the evening, and he brings with him a bag containing water, snacks and even an English language newspaper. After my period of isolation and inwardly cursing what feels to me like the selfishness of fellow passengers for a few days, it feels strange to encounter someone who appears to care about my wellbeing.

On my desk are several neatly arranged envelopes, each with my name printed on it: a note from the general manager welcoming me to the hotel, a note from the food and beverage manager with the offer of a complimentary cocktail, and a courier envelope from a local travel agent with a ticket to Hong Kong that I've forgotten I don't have. Perfect. Then the usual ritual of bathing and removing the accumulated grime from the journey. This feels like a good moment to remove my beard, too, so I cut it away with blunt scissors before shaving twice. They probably won't recognise me in reception, but at least I now look more like my passport photograph. Settling in, I can't stop myself from peering out of the little hole in the door of my room to see if there are any guests smoking in the corridor. I'm clearly still decompressing. The final act of the transformation is to carefully seal my contaminated flip-flops in a plastic bag and dispose of them.

Wandering the streets in the neighbourhood of the hotel the next day, Guangzhou feels like no other city in mainland China. It's much more like Hong Kong, and I can't spot anything much more than a few years old. Its inhabitants are now 21st-century consumerists who could be living in any big Asian city. In a moment of nostalgia, I try to find the hotel that I'd stayed in on my last visit here, in about 1990; then the only five-star hotel in Canton, The White Swan was built on its own island in the river. I recognise the building, but discover that it's now closed, awaiting total renovation. Hopefully one day it will become famous again, in the same way that Raffles is now seen as culturally significant in Singapore, or the Eastern & Oriental Hotel in Penang.

I decide that I will make myself look a bit more presentable for my arrival in Hong Kong. I badly need a haircut, and manage to find a place where two elderly men give expensive trims to expat businessmen. It normally takes about five minutes to cut my hair with clippers to a 'number 2' on the back and sides. But today there is to be no hurrying the process. The haircut turns out to only be part of the experience, and various contraptions are brought out from cupboards to massage my shoulders, steam-clean my face and remove debris from my ears. Complete with a choice of Cantonese reading material and a cup of green tea, this experience takes a couple of hours.

The city proves too big for me to enjoy. Or at least I don't find it easy to enjoy the part of it that I'm staying in; rents must be too high for this area to sustain any interesting restaurants, and it's devoid of the kind of little old shops that I love spending time in. Instead it's made up of office blocks, embassies and chain sandwich bars where office workers spend about five minutes eating before scurrying back to their desks. I waste a lot of time in taxis travelling to restaurants that are long gone. I visit markets that sell only western things. It's a bit depressing, so I do what I do when I feel let down by a city. I retreat to the health club in my hotel.

The lift doors on the 17th floor open to reveal that the health club reception has been created in homage to a James Bond villain's lair. The whole space is covered in rough granite, and a small waterfall flows behind the desk to a walkway over a pond. I can't see any crocodiles, but this doesn't mean that they aren't there. Check-in is conducted by suntanned staff dressed in well-pressed tennis outfits. There are no locker keys here; instead I'm presented with a smartcard and a number. A young man with an implausibly white smile shows me through into the men's changing room. I never feel very comfortable in communal changing rooms, something that I think extends from experiences at boarding school, where towel flicking, soap throwing and communal bathing in dirty water were a part of everyday life. Leaving my glasses in the locker, and dressed in just a fluffy towel, I head out the changing room door in search of the sanctuary of the steam room. I can't see too well without my specs, but it's soon pretty obvious that I'm actually back at reception, where the team behind the desk quickly usher me back inside.

Steam room etiquette varies around the world. I always like to say hello to people when I enter, even though I often can't even see them through the thick mist. You just have to assume they're there until your eyes adjust. It's a place where you can often meet people that you might not otherwise get to chat with – but today there are just a couple of Chinese businessmen here finalising a deal, so the conversation in English is minimal. Then there is the game of who will survive the longest. I like to turn the temperature up to maximum and pretend that this is completely normal for me. My opponent's resolve often quickly fades at this point, and they leave in search of a shower to cool down. Here, I play this game a couple of times, and then find a couch to settle on in a quiet room where I fall asleep without making any attempt to do so.

Several hours later and back in my room I gaze out the window onto the Blade Runner world. Daylight has been replaced by artificial light. Huge digital billboards are visible across the city from miles away, probably even from a low Earth orbit. It's time to pack my bags again. But this time I can lighten the load. I don't need any rations for the next leg, so I can travel with just two bags. I never like to leave packing to the last minute. Once I have proved to myself that I can squeeze everything in, I head out to explore the city for a final night.

Nostalgia drives me to seek a couple of the places that I remember from nearly 25 years ago. The big prize tonight is to find a nightclub I remember called The Time Tunnel. Based on a 1960s American TV show, the idea was that two scientists become lost in a science experiment and move between the past and the future. I too wish to become lost in the corridors of time once more, as it had been quite a lot of fun last time. So, using a slightly dodgy map provided by the hotel concierge, I walk up and down the street looking for the tell-tale entrance way, the tunnel to another time – but it's not there any more. I think I've found the right spot, and I have that feeling that I recognise something about it, but one Chinese city street looks quite like another, and I can't be too sure. Instead I have to console myself with a big bowl of noodles in a busy Vietnamese restaurant nearby. The beer is cold, and there is even some entertainment provided by one of those three-piece Filipino bands that can be found in hotel bars across Asia. The singer is pretty but looks bored, and the guitarist has talent, but it is the keyboard player that shines. With thick plastic glasses and a cheap suit he doesn't look like an emerging rock star, but as the set goes on he begins to wildly lift his keyboard off its stand and plays it like he is auditioning for a part in The Blues Brothers. Luckily for the other diners, I decide to leave before the karaoke starts, and take an early night. This time tomorrow I hope to be in Hong Kong.

I hop into an empty bus just 37 minutes before my train is due to depart. I haven't spotted that my ticket suggests arriving at the Guangdong East station a minimum of 45 minutes prior to departure – but fortunately the queues are short today. Having ascended a long escalator to reach the international waiting room, I complete the Chinese exit formalities and customs before boarding the train. If I had known about the red tape I would have given myself some more time to be safe, but I was blissfully unaware of the process until I arrived at the station. Fortunately, no one seems too fussed, and the place has the feel of a provincial airport departure lounge. My train today is the Z283. It's one of two different direct train types that operate between Guangzhou and Hong Kong on the Guangdong through train line. A recent addition to this route is a separate high-speed line that connects Hong Kong with destinations as far away as Beijing, so a journey that once took a couple of days is now possible in just a matter of hours. But today I'm more than happy to be on the slow line. At just under two hours it's not a long journey, and the train is a double decker, my first duplex on this trip. And even though it's the slower train, on the first part of the journey, through what is now the major conurbation of Shenzhen, it will be travelling at close to 160 kph.

Only once the train is at the platform and ready to depart are passengers allowed out of the waiting room. This KTT train, operated by MTR (the mass transit rail network) of Hong Kong, is not quite as swish as the other type, but the timings make it more suitable for my journey. Having treated myself to a seat in first class, I'm mildly annoyed to discover that there are an even plusher pair of 'executive class' carriages – first class is really just the ordinary class on this train. There are only a few passengers on the top deck, though, so I find a better seat than the one I have a reservation for, and spread myself out over a couple of seats and a table facing our direction of travel. I haven't been on an open-plan day train since Berlin, and it feels rather odd to be sharing the space with fellow passengers. But I quickly adjust to this, settle back and read the on-board magazine. Soon we are whizzing along at full speed. The hot sun streaming through the windows feels good and lifts my mood. Another of the tricks to successful long-range rail adventure is to mix things up a bit. Slow trains, fast trains, long journeys, short trips. After the slog from Lhasa, this is fun!

The journey to Hong Kong's Hung Hom terminus is non-stop (though there's a slow trundle through the frontier station at Lo Wu), and I feel comfortable leaving my bags unattended by my seat whilst I take a look around the train. Deciding to confront my well-founded fear of Chinese train hygiene, I also decide to try out the toilet. It turns out to be very shiny inside and there some important notices on the wall in several languages. The one I like the most proclaims that there is a

5000 RMB fine for smoking, and my second favourite is a cleaning inspection rota, containing a telephone number to call in the event of any dissatisfaction. I make a note of it in case I ever need it in the future. Like the train from Lhasa, this is a Z-class train – but there is absolutely no spitting or smoking going on here.

The final stretch of the line from the New Territories into Kowloon is underground, and getting off the train at a dimly lit platform I walk down towards the front of the train to take a picture to mark the occasion of my arrival. I don't get far before being apprehended, though, and I have to convince security I'm a railway enthusiast, and not a terrorist or asylum seeker. Job done, I join the back of the queue at immigration, but it doesn't take long to get through, and I'm in a taxi headed downtown before you can say 'Hong Kong Phooey'. My driver looks like he might have other things on his mind. He has configured a 'head up' display of at least five mobile phones and map devices stuck to the windscreen in front of his field of view, each hooked up to brightly coloured power cables; a bet on the horses at Happy Valley, a debt for equity swap deal on the Hong Kong Stock Exchange, and maybe what's on local TV tonight are all coming through thick and fast in Cantonese.

The reception area of my hotel is a busy place. I can't help but listen in to the conversations of the staff with the people in front of me in the queue to check in: 'There are no rooms available. Come back in a couple of hours.' The man behind the desk is immaculately dressed and his suit is cut perfectly; no doubt the hotel regard him as an extension of their brand and demand sartorial perfection. Prepared for disappointment, I smile and pass my card over the polished mahogany desk. A few taps on his discreetly hidden screen, and he tells me that my room isn't available right now, but he has a better room with a harbour view. Would that be okay? Have the jungle drums been beating about my rail adventures?

The carpet in the elevator has the word 'Saturday' woven into the Chinese pattern. I idly wonder whether it'd be worth catching the lift at 11.59 pm to see how promptly it gets changed each day. I bet it's done with military precision here, maybe even a small ceremony. I love the attention the to detail of this place. It amazes me just how far business hotels will go to make their rooms beyond perfect. At the desk in my room is a little wooden hatch concealing several plug sockets, each pre-loaded with international adaptors to cover almost any possible connection. In the drawer to one side is a little stationery kit, complete with fluorescent pens, stapler and sticky tape. I suspect someone checks the number of staples in the stapler each day and tests the pens, but it's only a hunch.

Before I can relax and consider the final part of my journey, I need to resolve some kit issues. First of all, I find the futuristic Apple store in Canton Road, a street where anything seems possible. Foot massage emporiums compete with tailors and camera shops on the lower floors of the otherwise drab neon-clad buildings. Upstairs in the surgical and soothing whiteness of the temple of Steve Jobs, the diagnosis is that I need a new iPad; the mains port has been deep-fried by the electric shock in Lhasa. They offer to replace my device on the spot and help me transfer its contents. Then I visit the nearby Victorinox store and tell the story of the loss of my favourite penknife. The staff listen with sympathy and a sales lady opens a large drawer and fishes out exactly what I need, a black coloured Climber model identical to the one confiscated when I was leaving Lhasa. She even finds me a tiny screwdriver for fixing your glasses, which screws into the knife's bottle opener. With the happy feeling that my kit is once again back in good order, I head back to my base at the other end of Kowloon.

I'm about to descend into a nearby MTR station when I spot an intriguing sign above an elec-tronics store. It says 'Reptile World' and has a cartoon picture of a smiling crocodile. Is it a restaurant or a pet shop? I have to find out. Up a nondescript flight of stairs and into a cramped room full of glass tanks. From behind the glass hundreds of eyes stare at me. It's a pet shop. The owner, appearing from behind a tank of lively geckos, asks me what I'm after. I try to explain that I'm just looking without revealing why I'm here. He looks at me with some suspicion. I don't think he gets many drop-in visitors without a reptile purchase in mind. Or maybe he's used to confronting disappointed diners who fancied a reptilian feast. On the way out I nod in the embarrassed way that you do when you haven't bought anything in a shop that you have mistakenly found yourself in.

On the street corner a man starts trying to sell me a good deal on a new suit and offers to throw in several free shirts. His technique relies on the western politeness that you will reply to his offer. To him, even a 'no' is a buying signal. But today I manage to ignore him completely and duck past him down the clean concrete stairs into the station. Hong Kong's MTR is a joy to use; the subterranean world in front of me has signs in English, and clear colourful maps. The place is spotlessly clean. Everything seems calm and ordered, and with the swipe of an Octopus card I'm through the barrier where miles of escalators and moving walkways transport passengers to platforms. I love the names of the stations, a mixture of the city's colonial past and its Chinese past and present. First opened in the late 1970s and continually expanding, its lines now reach out to the new airport and right across the New Territories. The only exception I make to using the MTR is to switch to the Star Ferry whenever I'm crossing the harbour between the island side and Kowloon. Nothing beats that view of the skyline, especially at night.

Parts of downtown Kowloon today still look quite similar to the way they did when I was first here. But now, back on the street, I don't immediately recognise my surroundings. I must have come out the wrong exit of the station. Being lost, though, can be liberating and I decide to explore a little. The area is packed with signs for foot massage parlours. Right on cue, a lady appears at my side. 'You wan' massage?' She thrusts a leaflet into my hand. It has pictures of big comfy chairs in palatial-looking rooms. 'Very good for you, Mister.' A moment's hesitation to consider slumping into one of those chairs, and she has me hooked. She leads me up a dingy staircase into a small boutique that bears no resemblance to the pictures in the leaflet. The chairs are the plastic-covered reclining type that you find across foot massage places across Asia. She leads me to one by the window, switches on the air conditioning, and makes me some tea. I don't get to drink it though; I'm so comfortable in that chair that I fall asleep almost immediately. By the time I wake I have had a one-hour massage, a pedicure and a manicure. A cold towel, a reasonable bill, and I'm fit for Hong Kong again.

Retracing my steps back to the MTR station in the twilight, I see the neon signs coming to life and suggesting a wilder nightlife than one might expect here. This part of Kowloon featured in one of my favourite James Bond films of the Roger Moore era, 'The Man with the Golden Gun'. Released in 1974, it features a scene at a girlie bar called the Bottoms Up club. Scaramanga shoots a businessman outside the club with his implausible golden gun and steals the Solex Agitator in front of Bond, who is arrested and taken away in a boat to Kowloon side. But he is of course already in Kowloon. It's a movie blunder. In real life the club was in a basement on Kowloon's Hankow Road until the 1990s, but it isn't there today. Round the corner from where the entrance stairs to the club used to be, I find a chair at the bar of an Irish-themed pub. There must be something very exotic about a pint of Guinness to the average Chinese businessman, as Irish bars are everywhere. A man bearing more than a passing resemblance to Donald Sutherland introduces himself, and insists I join a party at his table. I never get to find out the reason for the celebration, but it goes on in several bars and until the early hours of the next morning.

You can't come to Hong Kong and not sample its plethora of Cantonese dim sum. The locals know where to go, and you are best just finding one with a large queue of people waiting outside for it to open mid-morning. Now, over on Hong Kong Island, in Wyndham Street in Central, I join those waiting hopefully outside Ding Dim 1968. When I say 'hopefully', my hope is that it will open its double doors before the approaching rains arrive. When the owner opens up, I'm shown a table at the back of the restaurant, perhaps to separate me from the regulars. It turns out to be the perfect place to observe the correct customs of eating dim sum. There are no menus here. Just little wooden baskets of freshly steamed and fried objects. The etiquette is complex, but eating alone I don't have to worry about the order I do things in. But on the other tables I notice dishes being passed in a certain way, and thanks being made by knocking on the table with one hand. Chopsticks are left in careful positions to avoid bad luck or evil spirits. I'm not keen on chicken's feet or pig's trotters, but the pork and shrimp dumplings are absolutely delicious. After a couple of pots of jasmine tea, I pay the bill and head round to Causeway Bay where I have an appointment at midday.

Jardine Matheson have fired a gun in Causeway Bay at noon each day since the 1860s. Originally the gunfire was to welcome the arrival of one of their tai-pans into the harbour, but after a complaint by a senior British naval officer, nose out of joint, the gun was ordered to be fired every day. The tradition continues, and white-suited officials load the six-pound gun, and fire it by pulling on a lanyard. I know this area quite well; behind the gun is a tunnel under the busy Gloucester Road, which actually leads to the basement of the Excelsior Hotel. The Excelsior is also of more recent historic importance, not because of its distinctive architecture or its management by Mandarin Oriental, but because in 1978 it featured in 'Revenge of the Pink Panther'. Peter Sellers wasn't at his very best, but it was the last in the series released whilst he was still alive.

Feeling more like a tourist than a rail adventurer, I decide to walk round to the Peak Tram, the funicular railway to Victoria Peak. There should be a big sign by the ticket desk saying 'tourist trap', as getting out of the shopping complex at the top of the tramway requires a degree of skill and tenacity. But for the residents of Hong Kong, this is their very own railway to heaven, the highest point on the island, at 552 metres above the harbour. It's certainly steeper than the climb up to Lhasa, though, and at a 48% incline I'm in a seat almost at the angle of an astronaut ready for blast-off. From the summit if you are lucky you get to see the city in one massive vista. Eagles soaring above the skyscrapers, bum boats in the harbour and acres of cranes working to reclaim more land from the sea. Or I would have seen that today, if the dark clouds hadn't obscured most of the view.

My first day or two in the city feel a bit like an anti-climax. No one's here to greet me or say 'well done, old chap' or 'are you the only person to have ever completed both the Trans-Manchurian and the Qinghai–Tibet railways in one journey?' I walk the streets amongst throngs of tourists and locals who probably have no idea that it is possible to take the train from Edinburgh Waverley to Hung Hom. When I arrived in Hong Kong I was a little guarded about sharing my journey with the people I met, and when I did try to explain, the conversation was punctuated as much with 'why?' as with 'how?'; and 'Wouldn't it be easier by plane?' But I clearly haven't had enough of the rails yet, as the next day I arrange to take a commuter train from Hung Hom station on the east line up to Taipo Market in the New Territories. Situated only about five minutes from the border, it is perhaps as sleepy a town as it's possible to find in modern-day Hong Kong. My plan is to sample some slightly edgy food in local restaurants. The growth of Hong Kong is such that you now have to travel almost to mainland China to find the family-run places that were once everywhere. Many towns in the New Territories are already full of branded restaurants – but not Taipo. Here the chains have yet to arrive.

All you need is someone who knows where to eat. Cue Silvana, my Cantonese expert in local cuisine.

I had arranged to meet her in the ticket hall of Taipo station. Having fixed up the meeting by email, it was the usual drill: stare at anyone who might possibly be Silvana until they choose to ignore me or report me to the police. We find each other in the end, and hatch a plan. From a long list of exotic possibilities, we agree snake is going to be a good choice in these parts.

If you want to get a feel for what Hong Kong was like a few decades ago, go to Taipo. The people are charming, a community where people talk to each other. There is space for markets on the streets, and little traffic. I lose count of the number of places we eat in, but I learn all sorts of things about the local food. Most impressively perhaps, is my newfound ability to sex a goose by just looking at its head. I practise my new skill by looking at the carcasses hanging in the restaurant windows until I can get it right every time.

To say that my snake experience wasn't quite the one that I was expecting would be an understatement. The place Silvana has chosen is run by a well known purveyor of snake in the Hong Kong restaurant industry. I've been told he is in fact the go-to guy when the police have any major snake emergencies. But the famous snake man isn't here today, so I like to think he's on an emergency call out to capture a vicious python from someone's apartment in Sha Tin. We sit down at a little plastic table and perch on bright coloured plastic chairs, the sort you might find in a primary school classroom. Around us on shelves are dozens of bottles of something with snake organs floating in, and on our table, piles of chopsticks in a pot, soy sauce and chilli flakes in glass bottles. Like every mom and pop place in Asia, there is also a brightly coloured plastic pot stuffed full of paper napkins or toilet paper. If Hong Kong has an Ikea, I bet they sell sets of this kind of stuff. I amuse myself considering a Scando-Chinese name for the imaginary set, whilst Silvana orders me a beer. It seems like a suitably manly beverage to have with a deadly reptile.

I choose the snake soup to start, which comes in a small metal bowl and is served with dried lemon leaves floating on top. It doesn't taste of much to me, but the lemon leaves are a new flavour to my palate. Snake wine is optional, unless you need a boost of virility, in which case it's essential. I decide to stick with my beer. We order cobra for our main course, crispy and shredded. After talking to the waiter Silvana explains to me that we have to choose the cobra that we will be eating, and summons me to join her in the kitchen.

Through the door is a room with metal benches and steaming cauldrons. There are lots of knives, hatchets and saws close to hand. On the floor are a couple of metal mesh cages containing snakes. Chef opens a hatch in the top of the furthest cage from where I'm standing, and his assistant produces a long pair of metal tongs which he uses to pull out an unlucky reptile. The snake isn't very happy about this situation, hissing and flailing from the grasp of the tongs whilst trying to inflict injury on its captor. I do the manly thing at this point and hide behind Silvana, using her as a thin, but surely very tasty shield. Suspecting that the demise of the snake isn't going to be very pleasant to watch, I make my excuses and wander back to our table.

You can't hurry cooking a good snake, it would seem, as our dish takes a long time to arrive. In the meantime, a couple of little glasses of bodily fluids are presented to me, one of blood and the other containing something to do with its gall bladder. Silvana explains that this is great for the circulation, so I drink it down in one. It tastes revolting. Then she matter-of-factly explains that people have occasionally died when the venom of the snake has got into the wrong organs during its preparation. I drink my beer as though it may be my last, until the dish itself eventually arrives. Although I feel rather sorry for the snake, it tastes pretty good.

I'm both surprised and a little disappointed to discover that my snake isn't from Hong Kong or even from mainland China; there are now laws in place that prevent the export of mainland Chinese snake, even to Hong Kong. My snake today was captured in Indonesia, which seems a little crazy. Indonesia is home to some of the biggest snakes in the world, but in the same way as getting your asparagus from Peru back home, or your tomatoes from Tenerife, it feels less authentic.

As we are walking back to the station in the early evening, Taipo is coming to life with commuters returning home after a busy day at work. The train from Lhasa had given me some negative impressions of life in modern China, but here is a hugely positive one. Polite street vendors, unrushed shoppers, locals chatting on clean and tidy street corners. If I lived in Hong Kong, this would be the place.

I eventually have to say goodbye to Silvana and find a train to take me back to Kowloon. The two places bear very little resemblance. Outside of the brightly lit interior of the commuter carriage I can see little snippets of domestic life in the passing apartment blocks. Voyeurism, but all in the interests of trying to understand what it might be like to live here.

My last night in Kowloon is a hazy memory of expensive German beers and bar chat on the harbour front with investment bankers who find my world as weird as I find theirs. As the crowd thins out I allow myself a little time to reflect on another mission accomplished, this one definitely being the longest and most demanding that I have completed so far.

All that remains the next morning is the 26-minute ride in the express train to the airport on the island of Chep Lak Kok. This train is not only a fast and efficient way to reach the airport, but it's pretty scenic one too, as the line crosses huge bridges and causeways between the islands to reach its destination. At my first attempt I can't make everything fit into my big bag to check in for my flight and have to start again from scratch with everything laid out on the floor of my hotel room. At the bottom of a pile of crumpled clothes I find the white silk scarf that Tenzing gave to me when I arrived in Lhasa. I decide to wear it home in the hope it will protect me from the ravages of travel by air. It is perhaps the ultimate Mr Benn memento from an amazing rail adventure.

Acknowledgements

I would like to thank everyone who encouraged me to take the journey to Tibet and to write this book.

To Keith Parsons and Mark Hudson for their inspiration and help in shaping my plan. Theirs has been the perfect balance of motivation and support.

To Caroline Petherick, Colin Brooks, Olga Tyukova and Rob Woodcock for helping me to bring this book to life.

To Mark Smith at Seat 61 for once again providing the practical detail needed to commit to such an adventure.

To the online train community for railway inspiration, especially Wilbur Linsdell, Lindy Pyrah, John Blower, and Chris King.

To Sheila Manzano and the team at Three Little Birds PR for helping me to spread the word that long range train travel can be seriously good fun.

To Andrew Glenister and all the team at Real Russia for sorting out the tickets and the red tape.

To Mariosh, Lira, Rima, Sergei, Valerie, Andy and Rachel, Batman and Spiderman, Tenzing and Pasang for looking after me in times of need.

To the nun in the Potala Palace: I have recently had my eyes tested, and a change to the axis of the astigmatism in my left eye seems to have improved my vision.

To all the amazing people I met along the way who kept me smiling and welcomed me into their world. Thank you for making solo railway travel so rewarding.

About the Author

Matthew Woodward is a rail-based adventurer and writer. He has completed many long-range rail journeys from his old home in Edinburgh and his new home in West Sussex, reaching destinations such as Baku, Istanbul, Shanghai, Singapore, Tokyo and Hong Kong by train.

He writes for a variety of media and publications on train travel, and is a Fellow of the Royal Geographical Society and the Royal Asiatic Society. A self-confessed coffee addict, he carries an espresso machine wherever he travels. The Railway to Heaven is his third book.

For more information please visit

www.matthew-woodward.com

Also by Matthew Woodward

One:
Colonel Bogey

Thailand, January 2008

The third-class carriage on the train from Nam Tok to Thornburi was completely full. Not in an Indian commuter train sense, with people sitting on the roof, but rather that there was nowhere left to sit or stand in the shade inside the carriage. The passengers were a mixture of locals coming back from countryside markets and backpackers returning from the infamous Bridge on the River Kwai.

I must have been sitting on the wrong side of the carriage, as I could soon feel the sun burning the back of my neck. The locals always know which side to sit on; they even seem to avoid the indirect radiation of daylight where possible, let alone the power of direct sunshine on their skin. Coughing as politely as possible, I was ingesting a potent mixture of dust, diesel smoke and ash blown in through the open window as we chugged down the line in the direction of Bangkok. I love open windows on trains. Not just for the welcome breeze on a steaming hot day, but also for the way it allows you to directly sample the smells, the sounds and atmosphere of the world right outside. If you dared, you could touch a lot of what was going on without even getting out of your seat. Every now and again a single rotating ceiling fan delivered a waft of cool air in my direction, but it was an all too short-lived relief from the heat. Sitting on a sticky green plastic bench seat, I was surrounded by a group of kids I assumed to be students. They wore city clothes and took endless pictures of each other with the latest mobile phones available in Thailand.

Monks chanted prayers on the passing platforms, mobile vendors shouted out what they were selling as they moved up and down the train, and at each stop passengers bundled on, looking optimistically for somewhere to sit. In the corridor at the end of the carriage behind me was a man dressed in a dark military uniform. He wore aviator shades and sported a nickel-plated pistol on his right hip. I would guess from growing up watching films like Dirty Harry that it was a .357 magnum, but with a shorter barrel than the one Clint Eastwood favoured. It was a very old-school choice of gun, and a bit scary to think that if he were to fire such a weapon, the bullet would probably pass through both ends of the train and everything in between.

As we pulled out of the short stop at Kanchanaburi I could hear the guard at the end of our carriage asking to see tickets. His battle cry was 'Khaw do tua, krab; Khaw do tua, krab,' but he occasionally spoke in English too – just as well, given the number of farangs (foreigners) on board who spoke no Thai, or at least no Thai that a Thai person would understand. I count myself amongst those, as I can only speak bar Thai. I have a friend who only speaks golf Thai and another who speaks just spa Thai. If you are only going to learn a few words, you might as well make every one of them count in your lifestyle.

As the guard drew level with my seat I caught my first glimpse of him. He was a fit man in his thirties wearing a paramilitary uniform, cut in a very Thai way – a cut that would be impossible to wear with even the slightest love of beer. He wore a few badges, some medals, and what looked like parachute wings on his chest. Were he not the conductor of a train, I would proba-bly have mistaken him for a warrant officer in the parachute regiment. Glancing at me briefly he just said, 'Ticket,' and waited whilst I rummaged around in my bag.

My little white and green Thai rail ticket was crumpled and a bit grubby, but only a few hours old. I had purchased it even before the sun rose in Bangkok that morning. Handing it over, he studied it, and looked at me a bit harder as if working out what to do. 'No ticket,' he said. I pointed at the thing in his hand and reaffirmed my belief that it was in fact a ticket. 'No ticket,' he said. 'One way.' Had I known this I would have been feeling desperately guilty, but I had no time for such an emotion. I thought that my ticket had been good value at just 100 baht, and this explained why. That was six hours on the train for less than £2. But the full return fare was actually £4.

Feeling rather embarrassed I waited to hear of my fate. The students put down their phones and looked on with growing interest. The carriage seemed a little quieter now. The Thai women opposite who had been chatting incessantly were silent. I didn't look round, but I also considered if Dirty Harry might now have his hand on his hip, limbering his fingers, in case I was the punk who was going to make his day. But did I feel lucky? How would this foolish foreigner, who might even be a fare dodger, be dealt with? A fine perhaps? Thrown off the train? Escorted to Kanchanaburi police station?

Detention and deportation? My mind ran away with possible outcomes whilst he proceeded to get out a large brown notebook. This didn't look good. I thought about a bribe, but didn't see how this was going to be possible with so many people now watching us. Once he starts writing, I thought, there will be no going back.

I smiled at him and shrugged my shoulders in a way to look as passive and helpless as possible. I had often noticed the Thai preoccupation with saving face and avoiding direct confrontation. This didn't seem to make much difference today, though, as he quickly got to work on his paperwork whilst resting his heavy pad on the seat next to me. After a few minutes of careful scribbling he produced a stamp from his satchel (a kind of Thai Railways issue man bag) and franked the form, as if to make my fate official.

It turned out not to be an arrest warrant or even a court summons, but a special kind of ticket for people who had no ticket. I didn't have long to wait to find out how much this piece of paper was going to cost, as he tore the white copy from his pad and handed it to me whilst filing the yellow copy in his book.'You have ticket now. You pay 100 baht.' That was the same cost as if I had bought it at the station. Smiles all round – thanking him as best as I knew how for such an unforeseen situation:

'Khorb khun mark na krub.' I even offered a mini wai (the Thai polite bow), which he seemed to appreciate (or perhaps it was so bad that he just found it funny). Daring to raise my eyes now and look around at my fellow passengers, I wished that I also knew the Thai for 'nothing to see here – I have a ticket'.

With that bit of excitement over, I zoned out of the renewed din of the carriage and reflected on my day. I had spent the morning at the Commonwealth war graves at Kanchanaburi before inspecting the modern bridge over the River Kwae. Everything was absolutely immaculate at the cemetery. I had never considered before how the state of the graves would lift my spirits, but the devotion to neatness seemed wholly respectful and appropriate, and somehow made me feel much more positive than perhaps I otherwise would have been. As a repressed Englishman it took me some effort not to get too misty-eyed as I laid a Lady Haig cross on the memorial that I had inscribed with my failing hotel ballpoint pen, 'To the Railway Men'.

Back at the station, I found a songthaew (a van used as a share taxi) with its driver sleeping in the cab, and encouraged him with a few banknotes to take me along to the bridge. We set off, then after 10 minutes he knocked on the panel behind the cab, the signal for me to jump off, and waved manically at me as he sped off to find somewhere else to finish his lunchtime kip. I must have paid him far too much.

The street was swarming with frenzied Asian tourists buying t-shirts and souvenirs in the fashion of a closing down sale. I wasn't at all sure that they even understood what the Death Railway was. I had to escape from this, so I headed upriver on foot. After a few hundred yards I found a little restaurant on the river bank, where I could observe the bridge and gather my thoughts with a little more peace and tranquillity.

A man appeared from nowhere and before long I was enjoying a cold Chang beer and some fried rice, with only the occasional speedboat and an angry squawking bird to disturb me. I tried to connect my world today to this place 60 years before. Like many, my main reference point was David Lean's epic 1957 war film, which was actually shot in Sri Lanka. If you have seen the film you might remember the scene where Lieutenant Colonel Nicholson (Sir Alec Guinness) spots the wire where explosives have been planted on the bridge and comes down to the river bank with Colonel Saito to investigate its origin. I decided that my lunchtime location was pretty much identical to where Lieutenant Joyce had been hiding behind a rock with the detonator. Today there are no wires visible, and the train approaching from the direction of Hellfire Pass carries happy tourists rather than Imperial Japanese Army dignitaries. The bridge over the Kwae today isn't the same as the wooden one portrayed in the film, which was further upriver, before Allied bombs destroyed it. But somehow it still satisfied me to think that it was the bridge. At least it was Japanese-built, and parts of it dated back to 1944. The river was actually renamed Khwae Yai in the 1960s, to tie in with the success of the film. Despite this minor adjustment to history, what is very real are the graves of the 6,982 POWs buried a couple of miles away at the Kanchanaburi cemetery.

Back on the train I realised that I had been dozing off. I was coated in a fine brown dust and my throat was dry. We were about an hour behind schedule and the sun was beginning to set over Bangkok. The light is amazing at this time of the day and everything looks more moody and atmospheric. Getting off at Thornburi station, I brushed the dirt off as best as I could and bought a bottle of warm Coke from a street seller to lubricate my throat as I walked towards the river to find a boat to take me back to my hotel in Bang Rak. I nearly made it back without any further drama, but made the elementary mistake of standing on the stern of the ferry and getting soaked by the wash from a passing barge. Even the locals don't rate the water quality of the Chao Phraya river, and cower inside until the last possible moment when the boatman whistles that he is about to hit the pier, and it's time to make a jump for it.

Diving in the crystal-clear blue waters of the Andaman Sea later that week, I found that the Bridge on the River Kwai seemed to regularly drift in and out of my thoughts. Perhaps I had some unfinished bridge business.

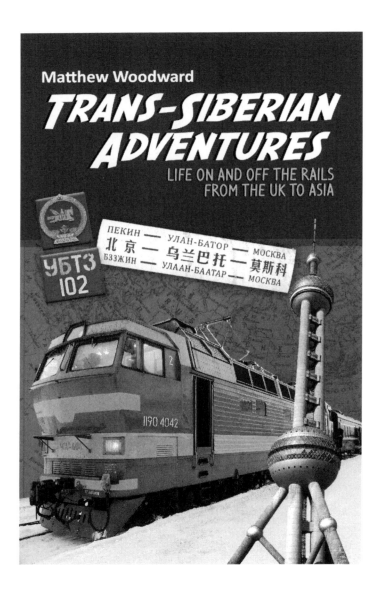

Prologue:
In Trouble Again

December 2012

Although the temperature outside is now well below zero, I am lying in the snug and sweaty darkness of a seriously overheated Chinese train compartment. After about half an hour tossing and turning I have a bit of a moment and finally lose my self-control in a high-temperature-induced panic. I feel an urgent and desperate need for fresh air. I need to do something, anything, so I grab my tool kit, get out some pliers and begin to remove the bolts around the frame that obviously keeps the window closed. There are eight bolts, and I remove them one by one and put them each carefully on my table like I'm working on an unexploded bomb. My compartment door is locked, so as long as we don't stop at a station I can continue my work unobserved by Li and Chen, my minders. The bolts are now all out, but the window still won't open. I push, shove and try and slide it in all directions. Nothing happens. Taking a break, and sitting on my berth I scratch my head and wish that I were a qualified engineer. Why won't the window open?

I realise that I'm going to have to admit defeat to living in a sauna. But then in a horrible single moment of mechanical deduction, the reason it's not opening finally dawns on me. This window is fixed shut and, unlike the windows in the corridor, has no opening part. What I have actually done is to unbolt the entire window and its frame from the carriage. At this moment there is nothing other than ice and grime holding the window onto the rattling and bumping carriage as we sway down the line towards Irkutsk.

One:
The InterCity Kid

November 1977

Like many children in Great Britain I owned a model railway from the age of about eight. It wasn't as glamorous as the ones some of my friends had. There was no Flying Scotsman steam engine with detailed Pullman carriages, no futuristic-looking InterCity 125 with working headlights. I was the hugely proud owner of a rather dull green 1960s Class 33 diesel locomotive and some goods wagons, described in the Hornby catalogue simply as the BR Freight Set. I'm pleased to say that this doesn't seem to have harmed me too much in later life. Back then, in 1977, just a trip to the model shop, its walls piled high with little red and yellow Hornby boxes, was all it took to make me giddy.

A journey on a real InterCity train was pant-wettingly exciting. The big Class 45 diesel trains used to thunder through my suburban station without stopping on their route to mystical and faraway places like Bedford Midland or Kentish Town. I was so obsessed by them that I used to catch a local train to St Albans, where the big trains did stop, and then catch one of those to London, speeding back past my home on the way. I felt – as best a ten-year-old boy could – like a real explorer.

There were ups and downs to being a junior long-range rail adventurer. I got kicked out of a pub in St Pancras station after putting Paul McCartney's 'Mull of Kintyre' on the jukebox. I assume was this was because I was under age, rather than the manager disliking Wings. On the brighter side I once met a school inspector on the platform at Mill Hill who thought I was quite special, and wrote to my headmaster to let him know about his prodigy.

I used to meet all sorts of people on station platforms. My railway list of who's who included actors Gordon Jackson and James Bolam. I wasn't a trainspotter, but I did spend most of my pocket money buying tickets to places I had never heard of, purely for the thrill of the ride. To me, trains were a clever combination of acceptable school-boy hobby and pure escapism. An old man with long silver hair on the television told me, 'This is the age of the train!' and I believed him.

As a student in the late 1980s I took advantage of the long summer breaks to explore Europe with a magical ticket called an Interrail pass. I joined the community of Interrailers sleeping on station platforms and various night trains trundling around Europe. For a £150 one-month ticket, I could travel north to Scandinavia, south to Morocco and east to Turkey, stopping at plenty of places in between. It was pretty addictive, and I just couldn't put my trusty Thomas Cook European Timetable down.

Sadly before too long, work got in the way and my cheap red nylon rucksack, battered sleeping mat and well-thumbed rail timetable were retired to the attic next to my train set. I felt that I no longer had enough free time to get anywhere that could bring back that long-range rail buzz. Somehow I got over my rail addiction and defaulted to travelling to faraway places by plane for those precious few weeks' annual holiday.

In 2012 I changed career and found myself for the first time with the ideal combination of resources to rekindle my love of rail adventure on an altogether bigger scale – some money in the bank, plenty of time and a large-scale 1956 edition National Geographic map.

This book is about my first ever journey across

Siberia. I have included some detail in the planning phase of the trip, as I know it will answer some questions that you, as a would-be Trans-Siberian traveller, might have.

It took me just sixteen amazing days to reach Shanghai. I mention this as many people can get three weeks off work every year, yet somehow the Trans-Siberian is still elusive. I find this a bit strange, as whenever I tell stories about my journey the response I get is that it is something that they have always really wanted to do.

Each year I return home older and wiser from my adventures, but I just can't seem to shake off the thrill of travelling to somewhere very distant and implausible by train.

Have you enjoyed this book?

If so, why not write a review on your favourite website?

If you would like to find out more about Matthew Woodward and his latest adventures, please visit:

www.matthew-woodward.com

You can also find him on Twitter at @OnTheRails and on Facebook at @LivingOnTheRails

Thank you for buying this Lanna Hall book.

Printed in Poland
by Amazon Fulfillment
Poland Sp. z o.o., Wrocław

48898325R00148

The Railway to Heaven

Also by Matthew Woodward:

Trans-Siberian Adventures

A Bridge Even Further